Connecting with God

A Guide to Prayer

Connecting
with God

Basic Bible Studies
for Everyone

HARVEST HOUSE PUBLISHERS
EUGENE, OREGON

CONNECTING WITH GOD
Stonecroft Bible Studies
Copyright © 2012 by Stonecroft Ministries, Inc.
www.stonecroft.org
Published by Harvest House Publishers
Eugene, Oregon 97402
www.harvesthousepublishers.com

ISBN 978-0-7369-5195-1 (pbk.)
ISBN 978-0-7369-5196-8 (eBook)

Printed in the United States of America

12 13 14 15 16 17 18 19 20 / VP-CD / 10 9 8 7 6 5 4 3 2 1

Contents

IIIIIIIIIIIIIIIIIIIIIIII

Acknowledgments

Stonecroft wishes to acknowledge Janice Mayo Mathers for her dedication in serving the Lord through Stonecroft. Speaker, author, and National Board Member, Jan is the primary author of revised Stonecroft Bible Studies. We appreciate her love for God's Word and her love for people who need Him. Stonecroft also thanks the team who surrounded Jan in prayer, editing, design, and creative input to make these studies accessible to all.

Welcome to
Stonecroft Bible Studies!

At Stonecroft, we connect you with God, each other, and your communities.

It doesn't matter where you've been or what you've done... God wants to be in relationship with you. And one place He tells you about Himself is in His Word—the Bible. Whether the Bible is familiar or new to you, its contents will transform your life and bring answers to your biggest questions.

Gather with people in your community—women, men, couples, young and old alike—and discover together what the Bible says about communicating with God. Find out how prayer helps you trust Him more and confidently relax in His love and provision for you. As you become closer to Him, your life will increasingly take on His marvelous character traits.

Each chapter of *Connecting with God* includes discussion questions to stir up meaningful conversation, specific Scripture verses to investigate, and time for prayer to connect with God and each other.

Discover more of God and His ways through this small-group exploration of the Bible.

Tips for Using This Study

This book has several features that make it easy to use and helpful for your life:

- The page number or numbers given after every Bible reference are keyed to the page numbers in the *Abundant Life Bible*. This handy paperback Bible uses the New Living Translation, a recent version in straightforward, up-to-date language. We encourage you to obtain a copy through your group leader or at stonecroft.org.

- Each chapter ends with a section called "Thoughts, Notes, and Prayer Requests." Use this space for notes or for thoughts that come to you during your group time or study, as well as prayer requests.

- In the back of the book you will find "Journal Pages"—a space available for writing down how the study is changing your life or any other personal thoughts, reactions, and reflections.

- Please make this book and study your own. We encourage you to use it and mark it in any way that helps you grow in your relationship with God!

If you find this study helpful, you may want to investigate other resources from Stonecroft. Please take a look at "Stonecroft Resources" in the back of the book or online at **stonecroft.org/store.**

stonecroft.org

1

The Purpose of Prayer

Those persons who know the deep peace of God,
the unfathomable peace that passeth all understanding,
are always men and women of much prayer.

—R.A. Torrey

Two young Americans were traveling in China. One day, craving a taste of home, they went to a McDonald's for a chocolate shake. While they were standing in line, one of the men, Jeff, discovered his wallet was missing. Everything he needed was in that wallet—his passport and visa, 2300 American dollars, and all of his required travel records. He grabbed his friend's arm in panic. "My wallet's gone! We've got to find it!"

His friend tried to calm him, telling him he'd pray while Jeff retraced his steps, but Jeff resisted, "No—you've got to help me! We've both got to go look for it, *now!*" His friend looked around and spotted a bench. "Look, the best thing I can do for you right now is to pray. I'm going over to that bench right there, and I'm going to sit there and pray while you look for your wallet."

So while Jeff headed down the street in search of the missing wallet, his friend sat on the bench and prayed. The streets were clogged with people, and Jeff pushed urgently through the crowd, going into all the shops they had visited. His Mandarin was limited, and the shop owners didn't speak English—and with every shake of the head his panic increased. Finally, on the corner of two busy streets, he stopped to pray. "God, you know where these things are. Only you can find them for me."

When he looked up, he saw a traffic officer standing in the middle of the intersection, dressed in an olive uniform with a bright white sash across his chest and around his waist. Jeff had passed countless similar officers in his search, but he somehow knew this one could help him. He dashed into the intersection, and the officer waved him back. Jeff ignored the signal, dodging cars and bicycles, determined to reach the man. The officer waved him back more urgently, but Jeff persisted. When he got to him, he tried to explain his predicament, but like the shop owners, the officer didn't speak English.

Near despair, Jeff felt a tug on his arm. Looking down he saw a little girl dressed in a plaid school uniform. "Can I help you, sir?" she asked in classroom English.

"I've lost my wallet," Jeff said. "It's blue. It has my passport and a large amount of money in it." The little girl turned and translated to the traffic officer. Suddenly the man's eyes lit up. Without hesitation, he left his post and dashed across the street, Jeff close at his heels. He hurried down a side street—one Jeff had never been on—to a small watch-repair stand. An aged man sitting on a bench rose to greet them. The officer talked briefly to the man, who then reached behind his bench and pulled out the wallet.

"Praise God!" Jeff cried in huge relief. He turned to thank the little girl who'd helped him, but she was nowhere to be seen.[1]

Prayer

Father, you are my refuge and shelter. I love you and trust in your name. You rescue me and protect me. When I call on you, you will answer. You will be with me in trouble and you will rescue me (Psalm 91:1,14-15, page 456).

Prayer Is Communication

God answers the prayers of His people. *Always.* Sometimes His answers are so soft you are aware of them only after the fact. Sometimes they are so incredible they literally drop you to your knees in gratitude and relief. But into every answer is woven this unchangeable truth: There is no power on this earth—absolutely no power— that is equal to God. And prayer connects us with Him, the One who penetrates the impenetrable, reaches the unreachable, and destroys the indestructible. He is the One who has toppled nations and found lost car keys; He has channeled tornados and soothed crying babies. Prayer connects us to His very heart and mind.

Connecting with God is a journey of discovery into communication with our almighty, all-powerful God, and I'm glad we're taking it together.

To get started, write down how you define the word *communication.* Making my thoughts of pleasure or need known to another. exchange ideas Communication is a dialogue not a monologue

Google defines it as "the imparting or exchanging of information or news." Webster adds that it can mean "personal rapport." I like the picture that *exchanging* portrays—emphasizing the two-way, back and forth aspect of communication in which both parties speak and both parties listen. And the word *rapport* underscores the idea of being personally involved.

Communication is instinctive to all living beings, connecting them by whatever means God has designed. Creatures that are isolated decline and die. There are amazing stories of prisoners of war who have developed means of communication through intricate combinations of taps. Their communication has become the lifeline that connects them, in spite of the impenetrable cell walls that have kept them physically isolated.

Prayer is the means by which we connect with God in an intensely personal way. No other created being has been given this privilege. The need to connect with God is designed into us, so since the beginning of time people have prayed. People searching desperately for Him pray to all manner of things—nature, animals, images of stone or wood, even other human beings. Prayer is instinctive to all humans, but it is vital to God's children. What breathing is to physical life, prayer is to spiritual life. It is our lifeline—our connection to God.

Have you ever wondered, *Does God really hear me when I pray? How can I know He will answer?* Although you may have questions about prayer, don't let them stop you from praying! We don't have to understand prayer to pray. The more you communicate with God, the fewer questions you'll have about prayer, and the more vital it will become to your well-being. It will become a connection you don't want to live without.

When you hear the word *prayer*, what comes to your mind?

Praising God, and telling Him just where I stand or need

Prayer Is Connection

Perhaps the most important aspect of prayer is that it is a dialogue, not a monologue. The second most important aspect is its simplicity. There are no "rules" for praying, no specific wording or posture or previous knowledge required. Prayer is simply talking and listening. It's no surprise that God has made it so basic—He wants to communicate with everyone, even the youngest. In the Bible, prayer is described by such simple words as *ask, call, cry,* and *come*.

Prayer doesn't require "religious" or flowery language. It doesn't require a certain posture or technique. Don't become sidetracked by technique and lose sight of the purpose of prayer—heart-to-heart communication with God. He responds to the honesty of our prayers, not the eloquence.

Proverbs 15:8 (page 491) says that the Lord *"delights in the prayers of the upright."* Imagine! God delights in our communication with Him!

Think of when your phone rings and the name of someone you love very much is displayed on the screen. How do you feel?

happy.

Isn't it amazing to think that's how God feels when we connect with Him? But it goes even further than that. Is there someone with whom you talk more intimately—with whom you share your innermost thoughts?

What is your relationship to that person? Why are you willing to share your most private thoughts with them?

Trust, Mutual Love

That's how God feels about *us*! That's the level of communication He wants to have with us. And we have the great privilege of prayer, in which God opens His heart to us and makes us privy to His thoughts.

Prayer: When and Why

The disciples learned many things about Jesus as they spent time with Him while He lived on earth. One thing they observed was the importance of communication with His Father in Jesus' life. Read the following verses and note when and under what circumstances Jesus prayed.

"Through the ongoing discipline of prayer, we are brought into direct and intimate contact with the Father's heart. As we continually behold His glory, we are changed into His image. As He has constant access to us, He realigns our vision, recreates our desires, reproduces His heart. Powerful, earth-changing prayer begins in the heart of God and flows through the hearts of His people."

—*Jennifer Kennedy Dean*

Mark 1:35 (page 762)

Jesus went out alone to a lonely place to pray

Matthew 14:23 (page 746)

Jesus went out alone to pray

Luke 6:12-13 (page 786)

Jesus won up a hill to pray. He spent a whole night

Luke 9:15-16 (page 790)

enough food for thousands

Mark 14:32-36 (pages 775-776)

after anguished prayer Jesus said not what I want but what you want.

How do the following verses instruct us in when and how we pray?

Hebrews 4:16 (page 922)

Let us have confidence then approach God, where then is grace! and mercy

Matthew 26:41 (page 758)

Keep watch & pray, for the spirit is willing but flesh is weak.

Ephesians 6:18 (page 898) *Do all in prayer. Pray always for God's people " on every occasion as the Spirit leads. Stay alert & never give up*

1 Thessalonians 5:17 (page 907)

What do you see as being the key points?

*Pray about it all & don't give up
Be aware & stay connected.*

The concept of always <u>praying is very</u> strong, isn't it? Pray at all times…on every occasion…never stop…keep watch and pray. In other words, never stop communicating with God. Stay connected!

How well are you doing this?   *Fair. Help me do better*

The Bible gives many compelling reasons to pray. Read the following passages and note what they say.

1 John 5:14-15 (pages 943-944)

*We have courage in God's presence
we know He hears*

Ephesians 6:18 (page 898)

*Do all in prayer, don't give up
pray always for all believers*

Proverbs 3:5-6 (page 482)

don't ever trust yourself. In everything I do, trust God & put him first

John 14:13 (page 823)

ask anything in my name and He will do it to bring glory to the Father

It is easy to stop after the first part of the verse in John 14: *"Ask for anything in my name, and I will do it."* However, we need to read the entire verse and this includes the last part, which is an acknowledgement that whatever is done brings glory to God.

Which of the above verses did you find most compelling?

There is an interesting instruction in prayer in Matthew 6:7-8 (page 737). What does it say? *This is how you should Pray> Our Father in Heaven*

If God already knows what we need, why is prayer so important? *I don't forget He is the source & He wants to hear from me. Know His way is best & only He has the power*

It goes back to prayer being a form of communication. It's not just a means of giving God a list of our needs. It's how we acknowledge our dependence on Him. It's how we align our will with His, and it provides an opportunity for us to see His faithfulness and love. Prayer helps us to first become familiar with God and then intimate with Him. It gives Him the opportunity to demonstrate His power to do the impossible. Ultimately, our prayer brings glory to Him—it gives Him the credit for everything that is good.

Prayer Is Not Complicated

God is holy and righteous. He stands completely apart from us in His purity and absolute moral perfection. The thought of communicating with Him might seem intimidating or even impossible, but nothing could be further from the truth. Only one thing is required for us to talk to God, and that is a personal relationship with Him. When we accept Jesus as our Savior, we become a part of God's holy family. He actually refers to us as His children, and we have the privilege of coming to Him as confidently as a child comes to an earthly parent.

How does Luke 11:2 (page 793) teach us to address God when we pray? *Father, May your holy name be honored, May your kingdom come*

God wants us to view Him as our Father. For many of you, depending on your relationship with your earthly father, this might not be very comforting. However, if you were to write out your definition of an ideal father, what would it be?

Trustworthy, Loving, Honorable, loves and Trusts God, Has unconditional Love

<u>Your</u> words could describe God. He is everything you could ever want in a father and so much, much more. Take a moment and connect with God as your Father, and then ponder the assurance of His unconditional love for you.

As we approach God in prayer, we can relax and enjoy our time of conversation with Him. It is our privilege to talk with Him, child-to-parent or best-friend-to-best-friend. The more personal our prayer is, the more it becomes real communication.

In Luke the disciples asked Jesus to teach them to pray—they didn't say "how to pray" just "to pray." And that is our prayer for this study. *"Lord, teach us to pray."* Through this study, we will be considering various aspects and advantages of prayer that will help us learn to pray. But the best way to learn is to just do it.

At the beginning of each chapter you'll find a "Prayer Profile"— an example of prayer from the Bible. For this chapter, however, we're ending with one. It focuses on a prayer that King Solomon prayed.

Prayer Profile: Solomon

Background: Solomon was a son of King David and the successor to him on the throne of Israel. Biblical scholars estimate that he was about 20 years old when he prayed the following prayer. Read 1 Kings 3:7-13 (page 260).

What did Solomon pray for in these verses?

aware of his need. He asked for God's help to understand, have wisdom. Discern btw good & evil

Humble

also gave riches honour he had not asked for

Did you notice the humility of Solomon's prayer? At the beginning he acknowledged his lack of ability to carry out the duties of king, as well as his need for God. He not only asked for understanding as he governed his people, but he asked God to help him know the difference between right and wrong. His request was very wise, because right and wrong isn't always clear, is it? Can you think of a time when you needed God's help in discerning the difference between right and wrong?

What were the results of your decision?

How did God answer Solomon's prayer?

*He was humble but bold
God did all he asked & More*

 God was clearly pleased by the lack of ego in Solomon's prayer. He wasn't praying so much for his own sake, but for the sake of the people he would be ruling, God answered.

Did you gain any insight about prayer? If so, what did you learn?

I seem to be getting this same message about

As we continue this study on prayer, ask the Lord to increase His importance in your life, and the importance of connecting with Him. Regardless of whether you have communicated with God for only a short time or for years, ask Him to give you something new and fresh that will enrich your prayer life.

Personal Reflection and Application

From this chapter,

I see... God wants me to talk to Him! He wants me to come to Him and align my thinking with Him.

I believe... God does care about each thing in my life and how I'm responding. Often, I'm closer to Him can show me His thinking and power to do more than I even imagine.

I will... Go to Him even more and expect even more from Him and be a person He can bless others through. I will see life & others more clearly and love Him even more.

Prayer

Father, you have said I don't have to worry about anything; instead, I should pray about everything. You have told me to tell you what I need and thank you for all you've done. Thank you for your promise that when I do this, I will experience your peace, which exceeds anything I can understand. Your peace will guard my heart and mind as I live in Christ Jesus (Philippians 4:6-7, page 901).

Thoughts, Notes, and Prayer Requests

Family look to You with gratitude, as the source
of life, Wisdom, peace, joy, fulfilment,
faith, love, praise, and every good thing
in our lives

2

God's Power in Prayer

The diagnosis was heart-wrenching news: terminal cancer. Sarah was the "grandmother" of our church family and beloved by everyone. To imagine her not in our midst was unthinkable. The evening after learning of her diagnosis, our family knelt to pray. I struggled to form my words, longing to ask for a miracle, but anxious about my young sons' response should a miracle not happen. Even to my own ears, my prayer sounded weak and ineffective. Our five-year-old began to pray after me.

"God, please heal…" he paused and reconsidered. "Please don't let Grandma Sarah hurt…" Another pause. "God, please help her…" Finally he blurted out, "God, would you please just handle this?"

Perhaps that is the prayer God longs to hear from each of us—one of complete, sincere trust in His ability to "just handle it."

❦

Prayer

Lord, thank you that I can boldly enter your holy presence because Jesus has made a way in. I will come right in, sincerely and fully trusting you (Hebrews 10:19-22, page 926).

—————— *Prayer Profile: Elijah* ——————

Background: Elijah was an Old Testament prophet who continually protested against the rampant idolatry and corruption among the Israelites. As a result, he was in constant disfavor with the evil King Ahab and his wife, Jezebel. Finally, determined to settle the question once and for all as to who the true God was, Elijah went to the king and told him to assemble all the people at Mount Carmel. "Make sure the 450 prophets of Baal and the 400 prophets of Asherah are there as well," he said.

What follows is one of the most dramatic stories in the Bible. Let's turn to 1 Kings 18:16-39 (page 276) and read it, so we don't miss any of the details.

As you read about all the extreme actions taken by the prophets of Baal and Asherah, what thoughts went through your mind? Could you feel their growing desperation? *yes. They wanted desparately to be right. Willing to cut themselves so their blood flowed*

Let's step into this story. Imagine you are one of the Israelites and you have been waffling in your commitment to God. You've been dabbling where you know you had no business dabbling. Now you're standing here along with everyone else, both curious and nervous about what's going to happen. You watch as the prophets of Baal and Asherah grow more and more desperate in the face of their silent gods. You listen to Elijah mocking them. As the day lengthens, you continue to stand there, hungry and tired but transfixed by the futility in front of you. The prophets start cutting themselves with knives and swords and begging Baal and Asherah to respond.

What were your thoughts when Elijah began to mock them?

He knew their gods were not God so he was telling them the weak possibilities for their gods not showing up which would never be possible for the real God of the universe, all powerful as He is.

When the prophets of Baal and Asherah finally give up on getting a response from their gods, Elijah steps forward. Note all the steps he took in preparing his sacrifice (verses 30-35).

He went "over and above" so no one could ever even pretend for a moment that anything nor anyone but the True God of Israel had come in His Power & Glory and that Elijah was His true prophet

Do you see the extremes he went to? He did everything he could to create a humanly impossible situation where God could fully display His power. Can you imagine what was going through everyone's mind as he had them continue to pour water over the very sacrifice he expected to burn?

Now go back and reread Elijah's prayer in 1 Kings 18:36-37 (page 276).

What strikes you most about it?

That God Turned their hearts back to Him!

No pleading or begging, no wailing, no nothing—just a bold request: *"Prove today that you are God."* I think the last phrase of his prayer is very significant. What did Elijah want the Israelites to be convinced of, besides the fact that God is the only true God? *That He is loving and forgiving and want them to be with Him*

All God ever wants is for us to be with Him! Take a moment and tell God how that makes you feel.

It's almost too good to imagine God cares about His people so much

Now we get to the good part—oh, this is so incredible! According to verse 38, how long did it take for God to answer Elijah's prayer? *Zap!*

What were the specifics of His answer?

It was more powerful than any fire they knew about! Elijah prayed to "Lord God of Abraham, Isaac & Israel to let it be known thru this that You are the God of Israel & I am your servant. That he had done all this at God's word and that he, Elijah was God's servant

He prayed that God would hear him so the people would know "You are God & you have turned their hearts back to you again.

Amazing! Not just the sacrifice was consumed by fire, but even the stones and the dust! And did you notice the word *"flashed"*? This was no slow-to-ignite fire, even as wet as everything was. God wanted there to be no doubt in anyone's mind as to who the true God was!

What was the ultimate result of Elijah's prayer?

when the people saw it, they fell on their faces, said, "The Lord, He is God! The Lord, He is God!"

Take a moment and write a prayer acknowledging that God is the God of your life.

Blessed, Holy, Father, your power and your grace to your people is almost more than my mind can take in but my heart jumps for joy.

Throughout recorded history, both in biblical times as well as in modern days, it becomes clear that those who have been most effective for God have been people of prayer. For example, William Gladstone, an eminent statesman and prime minister of Great Britain in the latter 1800s, was a man whose habits of prayer were well-known to his close friends. When he disappeared for a day, they knew he was spending time alone with God, reading the Bible and praying. Abraham Lincoln, the sixteenth president of the United States, was also known to be a man of prayer. He once said, "I have often been drawn to my knees by the overwhelming conviction that I had no other place to go."

Opening Up Communication with God

Before we go further into this study of prayer, it's important to look at what makes it possible for us to communicate with God in the first place. Let's begin by reading John 9:31 (page 818) and Romans 3:23 (page 859). What do these verses say?

God doesn't hear sinners but anyone who worships God and does His will, He hears. None has opened blind eyes. /All have sinned & fall short of God's glory. v24 And are justified freely by his grace through the redemption by Jesus Christ

So - "All have sinned & fall short but are justified freely by His grace from Jesus Christ

Every person who's ever lived on this earth has been born as a sinner, because of the first man and woman's separation from God—spiritual death—through sin. Sin is any attitude or behavior that goes against God's way.

Our sin reinforces our separation from God, which can also be called a broken relationship. But because God is always calling us back to Him (as Elijah noted in his prayer), because His unconditional love is always reaching out to us, He provided a means by which we could regain a relationship with Him. According to John 14:6 (page 823), what makes a relationship with God possible?

Jesus is the "Way", the Truth & the Life. He is the only way to God.

We can be reconnected with God and have access to His presence only because Jesus Christ died on the cross and then rose from the dead. There is absolutely nothing we can do on our own to restore the connection. The ability to have a relationship with God is ours only because Christ made us right with Him. We can't earn this relationship, but without conditions, God paid an unthinkable price to restore us to Himself—the very life of His Son. Whether or not we take advantage of this opportunity to have relationship with Almighty God is up to us.

When we accept Jesus as our Savior, acknowledging the price He paid for our sins, God views us as His child. He becomes our Father—a perfect father—who promises to meet all our needs and help us to become everything that He always intended us to be. Have you taken this step to be in relationship with God? If not, now is a perfect time. Agree with God about your sins and believe that Jesus came to save you, that He is your Savior and Lord. Ask Him to lead your life.

There is no magic formula of words you have to say in order for this to happen. As we said earlier, prayer is simply talking to and listening to God. You can talk to Him right this minute. The following is a simple prayer written out for you, if you need a suggestion.

> *Jesus, I do believe you are the Son of God and that you died on the cross to pay the penalty for my sin. I agree with you about my sin, and I want to live a life that pleases you. Enter my life as my Savior and Lord.*
>
> *I want to follow you and make you the leader of my life.*
>
> *Thank you for your gift of eternal life and for the Holy Spirit, who has now come to live in me. I ask this in your name. Amen.*

If you just prayed this prayer, you are now a child of God. It is very important that you tell someone about the decision you've made. Don't keep it a secret, because you want your faith to start growing immediately, and other Christians can help you with this. (For more information, see "Know God" on page 129.) ?, Pg 131

Christ has made a way for you to communicate with God openly and honestly. Again, *don't keep this decision a secret.* Let a friend know about it, or tell the people in this study group. You will never regret this decision!

||||||||||||||||||||||||

Prayer is <u>more</u> than just asking God for help; it is a way for us to <u>know Him</u> more deeply and intimately. If you are wondering how you even begin to pray, you are not alone. Even Jesus' disciples had questions about praying, as we saw in the previous chapter. Read Luke 11:1-2 (page 793).

Isn't it interesting that the disciples didn't ask Jesus to teach them *how* to pray but to teach them *to* pray? When we first start out, praying can feel awkward and even strange because we can't see God with our eyes. But as you learn to view prayer as an ongoing two-way conversation with God that involves both speaking and listening, it will become more natural. Sometimes your conversation with Him will be affirming your relationship and expressing appreciation for all He has done. Sometimes it will take on greater urgency. But view it always as a <u>conversation</u>, a means of communicating—communion even—with someone you love very much, <u>listening</u> as <u>much as speaking</u>. Keep in mind that the prayer itself, the <u>words you say, is not the source of</u> <u>power</u>—it simply <u>forms the conduit for God's power to be released in</u> <u>your</u> life as your intimacy with Him grows.

God understands our initial awkwardness as we learn to pray and is eager to help us gain confidence.

Praying in Jesus' Name

John 14:13-14 (page 823) gives us some important insight into praying.

What does it tell us to do when we ask God for something?

Pray in Jesus' name - I think this indicates we believe it is what He wants

It's the name of Jesus that gives us the authority to access our heavenly Father's provision. You often hear people end their prayers by saying, "In Jesus' name, amen." These words are powerful, but they are not a magical formula you tack on at the end of your prayer to guarantee a desired result. The name of Jesus gives authority to our prayer. It is praying for the request as Jesus would pray for it. When we pray in His name, it indicates we believe in Him and trust Him, and that we believe we are praying in His will.

As an analogy, imagine seeing your doctor and receiving a new prescription for allergy medication. When the pharmacist receives your prescription, she confirms the doctor's signature. The pharmacist will fill the prescription, not because you handed it to her, but because she knows the credibility of the doctor who signed it.

> "The power of the prayer does not depend on the one who makes the prayer, but on the one who hears the prayer."
>
> —*Max Lucado*

When we close our prayers in the name of Jesus, it's good to ask ourselves, *Is this just a phrase I use out of habit, or am I really making my request according to the principles in God's Word?*

Praying in Faith

Read the following verses and note what they say.

Hebrews 11:1 (page 926)

Faith is being sure of what we hope for and certain of what we don't see.

2 Corinthians 5:7 (page 884)

My pride can ruin my real desire in prayer. Be sincere and real in prayer not trusting in anything good in me

Mark 11:22 (page 772) *Faith in God*
Believe He will do His will

Faith is an essential element of our relationship with God. It's
also an essential element of prayer. How would you personally
define faith? *Believing that God is able (Faith)*
and he do what is in His will.

What does Hebrews 11:6 (page 926) say about faith?
Earnestly seek Him
Must believe that He is & He
will reward those who
earnestly ask Him

This verse makes it very clear how essential faith is to our relationship with God. Did you also notice that God rewards us for our faith?
In every single step of our faith-walk, God more than meets us half-
way. He gives us every incentive to walk with Him.

Now read Ephesians 3:12 (page 896).

What is the result of our faith in Christ?
I can go to God with freedom
& confidence (and He will hear
& answer)

Boldly! Confidently! Isn't it wonderful to know that we can come to God without any hesitation whatsoever?

The eleventh chapter of Hebrews is often referred to as the faith chapter or God's Hall of Faith. The people included in this chapter were ordinary people like we are, but they were defined by their faith. They trusted God in spite of overwhelming challenges, believing He would meet their needs.

Part of having faith in God is trusting Him to answer our prayers in the way He knows is best. So often when we pray, we have a preconceived idea of how God should answer our prayers. That's not faith. Faith is trusting God's answer. God sees beyond the immediate, we don't. He knows what every day of our future holds. That foreknowledge puts Him in a far better position than we're in to know how best our prayers should be answered. We can fully trust Him, knowing He never makes a mistake.

Read the following verses and note what they say about faith.

Hebrews 12:2a (page 927)

Keep my eyes on Jesus who is the one who gives faith and grows it.

When we commit our lives to Jesus, He not only initiates our faith, but He grows it, makes it stronger, more life-changing. Again, it shows how God runs to meet us when we take a step in His direction.

Romans 10:17 (page 864)

Faith comes through hearing the message of scripture, the word of Christ

Where is the best place for hearing the Good News?

Reading the Bible and in Church

The more we are in the Bible, the more familiar we become with the trustworthiness of God and the bigger our faith grows.

Luke 17:6 (page 799)

If I have the smallest faith, I can have His power and authority (when follow Him closely and and do His will Knowing He is the Source of my faith as in Him)

Have you ever seen a mustard seed? It's very tiny. But tiny does not limit God. He promises to do great things with our tiny faith.

The important thing is not whether our faith is great or small, weak or strong. It is the object of our faith that is most important. The power source is Jesus Christ—not our prayers.

Our faith is not to be in our prayers or even in our faith, but in the Lord Jesus Christ.

The God We Trust

Read what the following verses have to say about the power of God.

Jeremiah 10:12 (page 581) *He made the earth with His power! Founded world by His wisdom stretched out the heavens by this understanding*

Matthew 19:26 (page 750)

Psalm 62:11 (page 440)

1 Chronicles 29:11 (page 332)

God, who created the heavens and earth, is the same God who answers our prayers! We have the privilege of talking to the One who holds all the galaxies together! Now let's look at a few examples of how God has demonstrated His power.

Genesis 1:1 (page 3)

Exodus 14:21-29 (page 55)

John 11:38-44 (page 820)

John 9:6-7 (page 818)

Think of a circumstance in your life that looks pretty hopeless. In light of the above verses, do you think it is beyond God's ability to answer your prayer regarding it? Take a moment and write out a prayer, asking God to increase your faith in this matter and to use His power to resolve this circumstance.

God's power is unlimited! God's love is unlimited. Our close and intimate communication with Him connects us with that power and love. Connected to God is an incredible way to live!

—————— *Personal Reflection and Application* ——————

From this chapter,

I see...

I believe…

I will…

———————— ☞ ————————

Prayer

God, thank you for opening the lines of communication with me. Thank you that *"the earnest prayer of a righteous person has great power and produces wonderful results"* (James 5:16, page 932-933).

———— *Thoughts, Notes, and Prayer Requests* ————

_____

_____

_____

_____

_____

_____

_____

_____

_____

_____

Elements of Prayer: Worship, Praise, and Giving Thanks

The story is told about a well-known Arctic explorer who became seriously ill while on an expedition. He was brought 50 miles to a hospital, where a missionary doctor saved his life. Later, the explorer said to the doctor, "Nothing I could ever do for you is great enough to repay what you have done for me. You have saved my life. But there is one thing I can't understand. You could accomplish so much more if you did not do all of this religious work and did not spend so much time in prayer."

The doctor just smiled. "If it had not been for prayer," he told the man, "I would not have been here, this hospital would not have been here, and your life would not have been spared." [2]

Prayer

Father, your unfailing love is better than life itself; how I praise you! I will praise you as long as I live, lifting up my hands to you in prayer. You satisfy me more than the richest feast. I will praise you with songs of joy (Psalm 63:3-5, page 441).

God invites us to bring our concerns to Him in prayer. He desires to have a close relationship with us. Our conversations with Him have many different characteristics or parts—just as our conversations with people do. Some parts of prayer are worship, praise, and thanksgiving. Another part has to do with maintaining a clean heart—asking forgiveness when we are wrong. Prayer also involves asking God's help for ourselves and others. These things are not a part of every prayer, but each is still important.

One very powerful part of prayer is worship. King David, author of many of the psalms, provides us with wonderful examples of worship prayers. He is the focus of our Prayer Profile this week.

——————— *Prayer Profile: David* ———————

Background: David was the youngest son of Jesse and was known for his musical ability. As a shepherd boy, he defeated the giant Goliath. He later became the second King of Israel.

Read Psalm 145:1-13 (pages 478-479).

How did you feel as you read through this psalm?

Did you feel excitement stirring as you read about God's greatness, mercy, and compassion? Did you feel your love and awe for God increase as you read? That's why worship is such a vital element of our communication with God. It draws our heart to His.

Which of David's phrases of worship resonated most with you?

In just these 13 verses alone the word *Lord* is used five times. When it is written in small capital letters like that, it is a name for God in the Old Testament. It is His personal name—often spelled out in English as *Yahweh*. It can be translated *"I am who I am"* or *"I will be what I will be"* (Exodus 3:14-15, page 45). While this name of God cannot be completely defined, we know He is our promise-keeping God who never changes. David's psalms of praise and worship are effervescent and intimate, as he exults in the majesty of his Lord. God delights in such worship! In fact Psalm 22:3 (page 422) says that our praises actually enthrone God! Isn't that wonderful to think about?

Take some time to write your own psalm of worship in the space below.

Worship

How would you define worship?

What are some things people worship in today's culture?

Someone once said, "If you want to know what you worship, look at your checkbook and calendar." How we spend our money and how we spend our time can be good indicators of our values or what we worship most in life.

Is there an area of your life that you feel you might be giving too much credence to? Write out a prayer asking God to help you reprioritize your life.

Worship is lifting our hearts to God in adoration as we come into His presence. It is focusing completely on Him and expressing our devotion and honor to Him. But do you wonder why we are to direct our worship to God?

Read Revelation 4:11 (page 952).

Why is God worthy of our worship?

There is no one greater than God. Everything that exists does so because of Him. He is deserving of our worship!

One of the ways to worship God is to reflect on His attributes— the characteristics that make God who He is. The Bible refers to God by many names. As you learn the various names, it can greatly expand your worship, because each name reveals something about His character. For example:

- Jehovah-Elohim means "the Lord is God"
- El-Shaddai means "the Almighty God"
- Jehovah-Jireh means "the Lord will provide"
- Jehovah-Shalom means "the Lord is Peace"

These are just a few of the names of God mentioned in the Bible. Acknowledging these names is a wonderful way to worship Him. King David often used the different names of God in his psalms of worship, acknowledging God's characteristics and what they meant to him.

There are also many Bible verses that give us insight into the character of God. Read the following verses and note the attributes they mention.

Romans 15:5 (page 868)

Romans 15:13 (page 868)

1 Corinthians 1:9 (page 870)

2 Corinthians 1:3 (page 882)

1 John 4:8 (page 943)

Take some time to worship God, focusing on one of His attributes that is most meaningful to you. If you like, you can write your prayer below.

Our prayer lives are transformed when we learn to truly worship God. Worship enhances our love for God and refreshes our spirits.

Praise

Another part of prayer is praise. Psalm 48:1 (page 435) says, *"How great is the Lord, how deserving of praise."* As we worship God and consider all that He has done for us, our hearts overflow with praise. Praise gives the glory back to God.

Read Psalm 100 (page 459).

What does this passage tell you about God?

Don't you love the three attributes of God mentioned in verse 5? He is completely trustworthy, isn't He? This brief psalm is a great one to memorize, so that these words of praise are always in your heart and mind.

It is easy to praise God when our lives are running smoothly. When our hearts are full of joy, our lips naturally speak words of praise. But

God wants us to also praise Him during times of trouble. An incredible example of praising God in the middle of terrible circumstances is found in Acts 16. Read verses 22-24 (page 845).

This is another great story that is good to actually step into. Imagine that you are either Paul or Silas. You have been doing what God has called you to do, and as a result, a mob forms.

What does the word *mob* conjure up for you?

In the middle of an angry mob is not where you ever want to find yourself. Even if you're focused on God, I'm thinking you'd still be experiencing terrible fear. Paul and Silas are stripped of their clothes, so they are exposed and vulnerable. Then come men with wooden rods to beat them. There's no place to run, and they don't even have the covering of clothes to protect them from the terrible blows. When the severe beating is finally over, they are thrown into prison.

Imagine their physical pain, their emotional distress. What do you think you would be doing at this point in time?

What thoughts would be whirling through your mind?

I think I would be asking God a whole series of questions that begin with the word *why*. "Why didn't you protect me?" "Why did you allow this to happen?" "Why did you let it go so far?" But if "why" ever crossed Paul and Silas's minds, they didn't let it stay there. According to verse 25, what did they do?

Can you even imagine that? *When we praise God, we become more and more aware of His immeasurable power!* When you replace your thoughts of despair or anger or bitterness with thoughts of praising God, you are stepping over into His territory, where nothing is impossible. And the impossible is about to happen! Read verse 26.

This is such an amazing story, isn't it! Again, step into the story. You're the one who's been humiliated, beaten, and thrown into jail, yet you resolutely praise God in spite of your horrible circumstance. Then miraculously, an earthquake shakes loose the chains holding you captive and swings open the door to your cell. *Freedom!*

What would you have done?

Personally, I would have seen this as the providence of God! I would have been out of that jail before the ground even stopped shaking. But once again we see the result of a mind that is fixed on worshipping God, regardless of the circumstance. Knowing the jailor would be held responsible for their disappearance, Paul and Silas refused to take advantage of their unexpected freedom. What is most remarkable of all is the fact that none of the other prisoners escaped either!

If you back up to verse 25, it says that all the other prisoners were listening to Paul and Silas as they worshipped God. How intriguing that must have been to them! Something compelled them to stay when they easily could have escaped. It seems that Paul and Silas's attitude of praise held everyone captive even more than the chains that had bound them. God is glorified when we praise Him—especially in difficult circumstances. It not only brings God's power to play in our lives, but in the lives of people around us. Read verses 29-34.

What was the end result of this experience?

Paul and Silas praised God in the midst of their trials. Their words of praise kept their eyes and thoughts on Him, perhaps distracting them from their physical and emotional pain. Their faith was in Him, and they knew He was in control of their lives and their situation. Even in difficult times, we can praise God for the lessons we learn from our trials. We can praise Him for who He is and for what He has done for us. We can praise Him for being the God of the Impossible.

Is there a circumstance in your life right now that could benefit from giving God praise?

Our words of praise remind us of God's unlimited power and ability as we acknowledge our own helplessness. They remind us of how trustworthy He is, how deserving of our praise. Our words of praise keep God in proper perspective—there is no one greater and more powerful than He is.

Giving Thanks

The last thing about prayer we're going to look at is giving thanks. Ephesians 5:20 (page 898) says, *"And give thanks for everything to God the Father in the name of our Lord Jesus Christ."* Giving thanks is gratitude to God for the benefits we receive from Him. It is the grateful acknowledgment of what He has done or provided.

Read Luke 17:11-18 (page 799) for a story about ten men who had a great reason to be thankful.

How many of the lepers were healed?

How many expressed their thanks?

Don't you find this story fascinating? Ten men were afflicted with leprosy—one of the worst diseases of that time. Leprosy was contagious, and everyone's fear of it so huge, that the moment you were diagnosed you became an outcast, forced to live away from the rest of the population. You couldn't be with your family, you couldn't earn a living, you couldn't ever again live a normal life. Whenever you saw people approaching from a distance you had to call out, "Unclean! Unclean!" to warn them not to come near you. Can you imagine a worse way to live?

The ten lepers see Jesus coming into their village and fierce hope swells within them. They've heard about Jesus. *They've heard He heals people!* They start calling out to Him. *"Jesus, Master, have mercy on us!"* they plead, knowing He's their only hope.

Jesus doesn't disappoint them. He tells them to go let their priest see them. They were probably confused by what Jesus said. You only went to the priest if your leprosy disappeared, so he could pronounce you healed, allowing you to move back into the village. But Jesus told them to go as they were. Can't you imagine them talking together, wondering what Jesus meant? But all ten of them decided to do what Jesus asked—after all, they had nothing to lose. And lo and behold, as they walked toward the priest's location, their leprosy disappeared! Gone! Healed! Jesus had answered their prayers!

And now the interesting part. All ten lepers were healed! All ten lepers were given back the way of life they thought was lost to them forever. But only one went back to thank Jesus.

How on earth do you explain that?

It seems incredible that only one took the time to thank Jesus, doesn't it? But how many times do we fail to thank Him for what He has done for us? So many of the blessings we receive from God go unacknowledged. What are some aspects of your life that you tend to take for granted?

Take some time right now and write a prayer of thanksgiving for God's blessings.

An attitude of thankfulness is extremely important to our physical, emotional, and spiritual well-being. What does 1 Thessalonians 5:18 (page 907) say about it?

Do you think this is speaking literally—that we are to be thankful in all circumstances?

"All" is pretty inclusive, wouldn't you say? It lists no exceptions for having an attitude of thankfulness. Why do you think God gave us such an encompassing instruction?

Remember that God is our Creator. He knows precisely how we work, how our mind processes life circumstances. He knows that if we will cultivate an attitude of thankfulness—regardless of our circumstance—it will break strangleholds of fear, grief, or bitterness. It will take the power away from the circumstances distressing us and place the power in God's hand. An attitude of thankfulness keeps our focus on God, who has promised He will never fail us or abandon us. Read Hebrews 13:5-6 (page 928).

When it seems impossible to be thankful, you can thank God for the beautiful promise in those verses. Because you are God's beloved child, you have nothing to fear.

A great man of prayer, Andrew Murray, wrote about having so much to do in one day that he had to add an extra hour of prayer! We can follow his example by acknowledging God in all circumstnces and making our thanksgiving a priority. When we are in communication with Him, He energizes us to do what really needs to be done.

Personal Reflection and Application

From this chapter,

I see...

I believe...

I will...

Prayer

Father, thank you that you are righteous in everything you do; that you are filled with kindness. Thank you for being close to me when I call on you...and for granting my desires as I fear you. Lord, you hear my cries, you rescue me, and you protect me because I love you (Psalm 145:17-20a, page 479).

Thoughts, Notes, and Prayer Requests

4

Elements of Prayer: Confession, Asking, and Intercession

His schoolbook was missing, and he had to turn it in the next day or he would be given a failing grade. My 13-year-old son grew more and more distraught as his search continued to be fruitless. Soon our entire family joined in the search—to no avail. Bedtime came, and as I tucked him in I suggested he ask God to show him where the book was. "God doesn't care about my schoolbook, Mom," he said. "Prayer's not going to help. I'm just going to flunk tomorrow."

"Let's pray anyway," I said, "God cares about everything." Begrudgingly he bowed his head. "God, I don't think this matters to you, but if it does, would you please help me find my book?"

He lay back on his bed and I leaned down to kiss him. "Uh, Mom," he said, a note of awe in his voice. "Look over there." I turned in the direction he pointed, and there on his bookshelf, in plain sight, was the missing book. "I guess God does care about everything," he said, grinning in tremendous relief and gratitude.

Prayer

Father, thank you for being with me and protecting me wherever I go...Thank you for promising never to leave me until you have finished giving me everything you have promised me (Genesis 28:15, page 23).

We may not understand the mystery of prayer, but we do know that when believers pray on earth, there is action in heaven. What an amazing thought! When we pray, God hears. In our Prayer Profile this week we're going to read about how God answered the prayer of another desperate person.

―――――― *Prayer Profile: Jehoshaphat* ――――――

Background: Jehoshaphat was the king of Judah and a man who believed in the power of prayer. When he received the terrifying news that three large, fierce armies had joined forces to invade his land, he was terrified. His army was small by comparison. They didn't stand a chance against the well-trained armies coming against them. What follows next is a remarkable story.

Read 2 Chronicles 20:1-12 (pages 345-346).

How does King Jehoshaphat begin his prayer (verses 6-9)?

O Lord God — you alone are the God who is in heaven. Worshiping

By worshipping the capabilities of God, Jehoshaphat was reminding himself of what a powerful God he served. Worship switched his focus from the impossible circumstance he was facing to the sovereign God who controlled the circumstance. Did you notice that he not only began by worshipping God, but he reminded himself of how God had protected His people in the past (verse 7)? He reminded himself of God's ability to rescue anyone who cries out to Him (verse 9) and finally, he acknowledged their powerlessness and need for

God's intervention (verse 12). The first step Jehoshaphat took in facing the impossible odds of the upcoming battle was to align himself and the people fully with God, who specializes in impossible circumstances.

Read verses 13-17 to see what God told him to do. In verse 15 God gives two clear instructions. What are they?

1. Dont be afraid

2. discourage

What is the reason God told them not to be afraid?

He is with them.

Isn't that incredible? It's not their battle! It's God's battle! Do you know what? God is saying the very same thing to you. Whatever battle you are engaged in right now or face in the future—it's not yours to fight. It is God's! Stop and acknowledge what God is saying to you. Hand the control over to Him, and let Him do the fighting for you.

Verse 17 reiterates the same instruction in even more powerful words.

What five clear directives does God give them regarding the battle they are facing?

1. Don't fear

2. go out

3.

4. Take

5.

It's important to note that God didn't tell them to just "stay home and let Him handle it." He told them to go to the battlefield and take their positions. He wanted them ready and prepared. He wanted them mentally and physically focused on the challenge at hand, but He also wanted them to relinquish control to Him. The relinquishment of control is essential to victory. God wants your unqualified trust in Him.

What area of your life do you struggle with the most when it comes to letting go of your control?

Tell God that with His help you are willing to relinquish control to Him. He knows how difficult this is for you, and He will help you. He wants you to experience victory even more than you want to experience it!

The next part of the story is my favorite part. Jehoshaphat employed a very unusual battle strategy. Read verses 18-21.

According to verses 18 and 19, what are the first two things they did before marching into battle?

1. *Bowed low & Worshiped God*

2. *Praised God w/a shout*

Don't you like the *"very loud shout"* part? You can almost feel their confidence in God build as they begin to praise Him, culminating in loud shouts. It's kind of like the rally cry before a ball game, isn't it? But now check out verses 20 and 21. What does Jehoshaphat do?

David listen to me

So how would you like to have been in that praise choir? As singers without weapons on the front lines of a battle, they were guaranteed to lose by human standards. *It's pure craziness!* Here they are marching to their likely death, singing, *"Give thanks to the Lord; his faithful love endures forever!"*

> Remember that this is a true story! This band of people is marching into a battle of impossible odds. Even though God has told them not to be afraid, because He would do the fighting for them, don't you think fear would still have been a huge issue? Wouldn't it have been a huge issue for you? How do you think you would have been feeling right about then?

What made the difference then, and what will make the difference for you today, is the praise factor. Fear subsides when you are singing praises. Now read the most exciting verses of all—verses 22-24.

> Isn't God incredible? Isn't He awesome? Did you notice the very first words? *"At the very moment they began to sing and give praise…"* What was the outcome of the battle? List every detail you see.

> Take a moment and write out a prayer of worship to Almighty God for whom nothing is impossible!

Do you want to live in the Valley of Blessing? Practice praising God, no matter what.

Confession

The story we've just read is truly incredible, and it's just one of many stories woven throughout the Bible to show us the power that is available to us when we are aligned with God. But there is an important part of answered prayer that we haven't talked about yet. Read Psalm 66:17-19 (page 442).

> What is important to pray?

As God's children, our sins create a barrier between us and God, and our fellowship with Him is diminished. Isaiah 66:2 (page 568) says, *"My hands have made both heaven and earth; they and everything in them are mine. I, the Lord, have spoken! 'I will bless those who have humble and contrite hearts, who tremble at my word.'"*

> According to 1 John 1:9 (page 941), what are you to do when you sin?

What does God promise to do if you confess your sin?

forgive

Whenever God reveals sin to us, we are to confess it immediately. Then we can experience God's forgiveness and cleansing.

When Jesus Christ died on the cross, He took the penalty for all the sins of all believers—past, present, and future. However, as long as we live in a sinful world, we need to be cleansed by God from the influence of sin in our lives.

> "The forgiveness Christians are supposed to seek in their daily walk is not pardon from an angry Judge, but mercy from a grieved Father."
>
> —*John MacArthur*

King David wrote a beautiful prayer of confession for his sins in Psalm 51:1-4,10 (page 436). What do you note about this prayer?

Are you holding on to any unconfessed sin in your life? This would be a great time to talk to God about it. If you like, you can write your prayer out below.

Asking

Another part of prayer is asking—bringing our requests to God. Read Philippians 4:6-7 (page 901). What are the specific instructions listed in verse 6?

According to verse 7, what is the result of following these instructions?

extend yourself when you think you can't

Don't you love the idea of God guarding your heart and your mind with peace—a peace that exceeds anything we can possibly understand? *What incredible love God pours over His children!*

Read Matthew 7:7-8 (page 738). What does Jesus tell us to do?

Keep asking, seeking, knocking

What picture does this passage paint when it talks about not only asking but also seeking and knocking?

The first thing this verse mentions is asking. God wants us to ask Him for the things we need. Read Philippians 4:19 (901) and James 1:17 (page 930).

What do these verses say about the way God answers prayer?

seek

The next thing Matthew 7:7-8 (page 738) tells us to do is seek. We seek to know God's will, and we listen to His voice for guidance. We seek His resources for our supplies. Seeking is asking with effort. When we pray, we are to be ready to do our part—to be obedient to God. Turn to Matthew 6:33 (page 738).

What is to be our top priority in seeking?

whoever asks - recieves
ask , seek, knock
He answers

In other words, align ourselves with God and His principles, His righteousness, first.

The final action in Matthew 7:7-8 is to knock. This action speaks of persistence. God wants us to continue praying until we know His answer.

God tells us to ask, to seek, and to knock, and He will answer our prayers. How He answers and when He answers is up to Him—it goes back to our relinquishing control. But He has promised He will answer, and because we know we are His beloved child, we can rest assured the answer He gives will be the best possible.

Intercession

The last characteristic of prayer we're going to look at is intercession—praying for others. Read Ephesians 6:18 (page 898). List the three things it tells you to do.

1. Pray in the Spirit

2. Stay alert to be persistant

3.

Intercession involves three persons—the one praying, the one being prayed for, and God.

A great example of intercessory prayer is in Ephesians 3:14-21 (page 896). Read what Paul prayed for the people who were part of the church in Ephesus, then list his requests on their behalf.

Did you notice how Paul's prayers focused on their relationship with God? He understood that their physical and emotional well-being hinged on their spiritual well-being. Who do most of your prayers focus on, yourself or others?

Filled w/ fullness of God

As we've already seen, God wants us to pray for all of our needs—including our physical and material needs—but praying for spiritual needs is where lives are truly impacted.

Paul's intercessory prayers were almost always for the spiritual needs of the people. Nevertheless, sometimes it is important to pray for the physical needs of others. In Acts 12 there is a story about a group of people gathered together to pray for a friend in need. Read Acts 12:1-17 (pages 840-841).

> You believe the sufficiency of God when you ask Him for the impossible.

Their prayers were answered in a dramatic and miraculous way, but didn't you love how the story unfolded? Everyone is praying for Peter—including, I'm sure, Peter himself. But when God answers their prayers, it's so hard for Peter to believe it that he assumes it's a dream. When he comes to his senses, he hurries to Mary's house, where the servant girl is so excited she leaves him standing outside. As for the people inside, it was easier for them to believe it was Peter's angel than to believe God had acted in response to their prayers this way, this quickly. This is such a great story, isn't it?

Have you ever been like those people who were gathered to pray and then were shocked when God answered?

Thankfully, God understands our surprised disbelief. Do you think perhaps He might even delight in answering our prayers beyond anything we ever imagined was possible?

Jesus gives wonderful encouragement about praying in Matthew 19:26 (page 750). What does it say?

Sometimes what we're praying for seems impossible, but nothing at all is impossible for God. *Nothing.*

If the solution seems difficult, tell God! Read Romans 8:26-27 (pages 862-863). The Holy Spirit is your personal Advocate. He has a major role in the vital matter of all prayer. He helps us in our weakness!

Have you ever been in such distress you don't even know how to put your heartache into words? *You don't have to know!* What do these verses say?

HS helps our weakness

Weakness can mean many things. Read Romans 8:23 to find out more.

What kind of weakness is described? Is it just the kind of weakness we experience once in a while, or when we have done our best and can't do any more? Or is it something all-encompassing?

Our bodies will never be free of sin and suffering in this life. There is never a time here on earth when we do not experience this kind of weakness.

What does this mean in regard to the help of the Holy Spirit when we pray?

Yes! Our Advocate, the one who pleads our case for us in all matters, *always* intercedes for us. We should still pray—in those everyday times, in those desperate times when we don't have the words—because our prayers keep us connected to the heart of God. But how comforting to know that God the Holy Spirit is always there as we pray.

The Spirit always intercedes for us in harmony with God's will for us. What does Romans 8:28-29 (page 863) say the result of our prayers and the pleading of the Spirit will be?

Everything works together for good for those

God created us to be in relationship with Him. He communicates to us through the Bible, and we communicate with Him through prayer conversations and worship. Don't allow yourself to be robbed of this vital aspect of your relationship with God. God Himself, the Holy Spirit, is helping you!

Helping Others Through Intercessory Prayer

Intercessory prayer is a powerful tool in helping others. Our prayers go where we cannot. There is no barrier our prayers cannot penetrate, no gate they cannot open. Not only can we impact the lives of people we know, but we can also impact the lives of people we have never met—through intercessory prayer.

Read the following verses and note who we are told to pray for.

Ephesians 6:18 (page 898)

1 Timothy 2:1-2 (page 910)

"The inner sense of compassion is one of the clearest indications from the Lord that this is a prayer project for you. In times of meditation, there may come a rise in the heart, a compulsion to intercede, an assurance of rightness, a flow of the Spirit. This inner 'yes' is the divine authorization for you to pray for the person or situation."

—*Richard E. Foster*

One area where intercessory prayer could have tremendous impact is in the entertainment industry. That industry greatly influences our society's moral code. Change that industry and you change our society. Imagine the impact if Christians committed to pray for people involved in all areas of the entertainment industry.

Another area where intercessory prayer is vital is within families. When parents plead with God on behalf of their children, it brings God's power to play in their lives and great things will happen.

Think about your neighborhood. All it takes for an entire neighborhood to change is for one person in one house on the block to intercede for his or her neighbors.

To be a person who prays for the physical and spiritual needs of others, it is helpful to have a systematic way of recording your prayer requests. Journal pages are included in the back of this book. Journal your prayers and concerns. Then record answers you receive from God. For additional prayer resources go to stonecroft.org.

Have you ever wondered if anyone intercedes on your behalf? There is such an exciting, encouraging verse that answers this question. Read Romans 8:34 (page 863).

Think of it! Jesus is pleading with God on your behalf! Jesus! Is there anyone you'd rather have pleading your cause? Stop for just a moment to think about this incredible truth, then write out your thoughts. *prioritize, knowing Jesus is interceeding*

There is a moving example of Jesus interceding on behalf of Simon Peter just prior to Jesus being arrested. Read Luke 22:31-32 (page 805).

We get a glimpse here of what goes on outside the physical realm in this passage, because Satan clearly sought permission from God to test Peter, but Jesus interceded on his behalf. How did Jesus pray for him?

prays & interceeds that his faith wouldn't fail.

Do you realize that Jesus prays the same thing for us? Isn't that incredible? But look at the next part of that verse. What does Jesus say?

Jesus knew that Peter was going to fail, and in the worst possible way—by denying he knew Jesus. Peter swore emphatically that nothing would ever cause him to turn away from Jesus, that he would even go to the death for Him. But when things heated up, Peter denied his friend and Savior not once, not twice, but three times! Jesus knew this would happen, and in His love for Peter He showed him that 1) He knew Peter would repent and return fully to his commitment, and 2) Peter would use his failure to strengthen his brothers. *Jesus assured Peter of his forgiveness and continued usefulness, even before he sinned.*

Oh, what unfathomable love Jesus has for us! How far He goes to draw us to Him and reassure us in our weakness. Jesus never stops pleading on our behalf—He never stops believing in us.

Personal Reflection and Application

From this chapter,

I see... I need to

I believe... God hears my prayers

I will...

<hr />

Prayer

Father, I pray that from your glorious, unlimited resources
you will empower me with inner strength through your Spirit.
Then Christ will make His home in my heart as I trust in Him.
Let my roots grow down into your love and keep me strong. And
may I have the power to understand, as all God's people should,
how wide, how long, how high, and how deep your love is. May
I experience the love of Christ, though it is too great to understand fully. Then I will be made complete with all the fullness of
life and power that comes from you. Now all glory to you, who is
able, through your mighty power at work within me, to accomplish infinitely more than I might ask or think (Ephesians 3:14-
20, page 896).

Thoughts, Notes, and Prayer Requests

Carols Derek — job
Byron
People back east Help them to
look to you

Bazaar $1,741 so our group gits $174.00

God Hears and Answers

Nov. 16, 2012

Martin and Gracia Burnham were missionaries who were held hostage by a Philippine terrorist group for 376 days. Throughout the months of their captivity, they relied on God to meet their needs in both big and little ways. One day Gracia prayed, "Lord, can you figure out something for me to use to tie back my hair?" She'd been meditating on James 1:17 that says every good and perfect gift is from God. She glanced down at the ground, and there lay a strip of black rubber, like from a bicycle inner tube. She picked it up, tied the ends together and joyfully pulled her hair back.[3] As mundane as her request was, God cared and answered her prayer.

Prayer

Lord, you are my light and my salvation—so why should I be afraid? You are my fortress, protecting me from danger, so why should I tremble? Though a mighty army surrounds me, my heart will not be afraid. Even if I am attacked, I will remain confident. Hear me as I pray, Lord. Be merciful and answer me! My heart has heard you say, "Come and talk with me." And my heart responds, "LORD, I am coming" (Psalms 27:1,3,7,8, page 425).

– Prayer Profile: Shadrach, Meshach, and Abednego –

Background: King Nebuchadnezzar had a gold statue made and arbitrarily ordered everyone to bow down and worship it. If anyone refused, they would immediately be thrown into a blazing furnace. In spite of certain death, three young men refused to bow before anyone or anything but God.

We read the story in Daniel 3 (pages 669-670). Let's begin by reading verses 8-15.

This story is a great example of answered prayer. Because these young men were well acquainted with the power of God, they were able to exhibit great bravery in the face of Nebuchadnezzar's threat. Didn't you find Nebuchadnezzar's inflated ego appalling? He clearly sees himself to be more powerful than God (verse 15). But the three young men's trust in God doesn't waver.

What do they say to Nebuchadnezzar in verses 16 and 17?

They don't answer to him & if he throws them into the furnace, the God whom they serve, is able to save them. "He will rescue us from your power."

That's bold faith in the face of death, wouldn't you say? How do you think you might respond in similar circumstances?

I might faint or beg him not to do it. But I agree I would not serve another god. I think I could do this, only because of God's power & faithfulness

Personally, I can hear myself coming up with some very creative reasoning—especially feeling the heat coming off that blazing furnace. I can hear myself telling my buddies, "You know, maybe we should reconsider. We'll be a much better witness for God alive than dead. And besides, just bending our knees in front of the statue doesn't mean we're worshipping it. God will know what's in our hearts…"

Shadrach, Meshach, and Abednego's trust in God remained firm though. They absolutely believed God had the ability to deliver them from the flames. However, read verse 18 to see the true depth of their commitment to God.

Their faith in God was not in any way dependent upon God answering their prayers as they wanted them answered. Their faith was in God—period. They trusted Him—period. It is an amazing way to live, and it can lead down the path of miracles, as you'll soon see. Read verses 19-23.

What struck you about this passage?

They submitted & were calm, I don't imagine those who tied them & threw them in needed to be strong. They trusted God

Put yourself in those young men's shoes for a moment. Imagine their terror as they are tied up and dragged toward the furnace. Imagine being pushed into the inferno that was so hot the soldiers who threw them in died! From their perspective God had chosen not to answer their prayers in the way they'd hoped. But then along come verses 24-30. This is so great!

Don't you love it? What an incredible God we serve! There are several noteworthy things in this passage. First of all, look again at verse 25. Isn't it interesting that Nebuchadnezzar suddenly recognized God, when a few minutes before he didn't even believe in Him? Second, look at verse 27. The facts surrounding the circumstance these three young men found themselves in was that they'd been given a death sentence by fire—a fire so hot it killed the soldiers who threw them in. However, the *truth* surrounding their circumstance was that not only was their hair not singed, but they didn't so much as have the smell of smoke on their bodies. God's truth is always greater than human facts!

> In what way does this story help you have the courage to trust God with the way He answers your prayers?
>
> *"Your Will Be Done" are not just nice words to pray, they are "the way faith in God is". I know this and believe it more that when I was young.*

The power of God surpasses our most earnest petitions. It is beyond our understanding. It is beyond our ability to measure.

> Do you think there are limitations to the way God will answer our prayers? Read Ephesians 3:20 (page 896), and note what it says.
>
> *All Glory to God! It is within His power to do more than I can even ask or think!*

How much beyond our expectations is God able to answer our prayers? *"Infinitely more!"* No request is too big for His power to meet, and no request is too small for His loving interest.

There is no pat answer for the way God answers prayers. He answers each request in light of His foreknowledge and His plan for the person who is praying. Sometimes, when we have such a clear idea of how we want things to turn out, it feels as if God is ignoring us. That's never the case though. Let's look at some biblical examples of various ways God answers our prayers.

God Answers Yes

In the book of Mark there is an example of an immediate answer to prayer, when the disciples found themselves in the midst of a terrifying storm. Read Mark 4:35-41 (page 764). Note the facts you find most interesting. *a fierce storm came up so fast but Jesus was sleeping! Jesus just spoke & the storm stopped! Calm. He wondered why they were afraid seeing it as having no faith in Him. (They were Terrified!)*

Do you think you would have been afraid, knowing Jesus was in the boat with you? Why? *Yes, I think I would but I'd likely have awakened Him as they did. Actually I would in the faith that He could take care of it*

How quickly did Jesus answer their prayer? *Immediately, just spoke and it was over. Its a little different now that I know He's always awake & aware*

Jesus had an important lesson of faith He wanted to teach the disciples. More important than stilling the storm was stilling the fear and unbelief that remained in their hearts. He wanted them to know that their dependence must be on Him for every *storm* that they would encounter in their lives. Jesus heard their cry and answered yes.

What is your favorite "yes" answer to a prayer you have prayed?

yes, the doctors told us they discovered what was wrong w/ Byron and it was just a matter of 3-6 mos and the liver would heal itself. We are wonderfully Made by God!

There is a reason God allows storms to blow into our lives. What does 1 Peter 1:6-7 (page 934) say?

Enduring many trials for a little while, these trials show my faith is genuine. more precious than gold It will bring

What results does God want when you encounter trials?

Genuine faith in Him to get me through it

Do you have an example of a trial you've experienced that strengthened your faith?

Not knowing what Byron had and just going to Jesus for help and asking many

Is there a trial you're experiencing right now that is challenging your faith?

I don't think of it as challenging but I guess it is, as it draws me to him knowing I am not able to solve it but he is able.

Tell God exactly how you're struggling, and then write a prayer of faith in regard to your circumstance.

Thank you Father for the realization you give me, that you know about it and won't leave me to go thru it alone. Help me to

There is a poignant picture of how Jesus loves us in the story of the storm. It was obviously a terrible storm because the disciples, some of whom had spent their lives on the water and had encountered many storms, were terrified. Storms are not quiet. The wind howls! The thunder crashes! The waves roar! But Jesus slept through it all. According to verse 38 (page 764), what woke Jesus up?

their shouting, asking if He didn't care

When we become a Christian, we are not promised immunity from trouble. When we least expect it, terrifying storms may break upon our lives. Inner storms such as fear, disappointment, doubt, or resentment may take us by surprise. No matter how fierce and terrifying the storm is, Jesus will hear our cry above the cacophony—we are that precious to Him!

God Answers No

Sometimes God's answer is neither immediate nor in the affirmative—but as hard as it may be for us to understand from our limited perspective, it is always in our best interests. Read 2 Corinthians 12:7-10 (page 888).

How many times did Paul ask God to take away his thorn in the flesh? *3 different times*

How did God answer Paul's request?

*My Grace is all you need
My Power works best in weakness*

What was the result of God's answer to Paul's prayer?

So now Paul was glad to boast about his weakness, so that the power of Christ can work through me. That's why I take pleasure in my weaknesses, insults, hardships, persecutions & troubles I suffer for Christ. For when I am weak, then I am strong!

Paul's attitude in <u>the face</u> of his unanswered prayer made all the difference in how he lived with his trial. He trusted God's answer, and his weakness became God's strength.

Think of a time when God answered a prayer differently than you expected. How did you react at the time?

*I kept asking until it was the undeniable answer and moved forward.
Even in a bad diagnosis things have gone better than anyone can explain for 40 yrs.*

As you look back, do you have a better understanding of God and His character because of this?

It is not easy but was not the end of the world as I feared.
I simply trust God

God Answers Wait

When we pray to God, He always recognizes our voice and our cries will never go unheard. Sometimes His answers come as *wait*. It's one thing when we get a clear answer of *no,* but the answer *wait* can be frustrating. It's easy to think God's not hearing us or not caring about our need.

Read John 11:1-7 (page 820).

This story is a perfect example of why we can trust God no matter what is happening. Mary and Martha expected Jesus to come immediately, because of the dire circumstances. Their brother was near death. Jesus could help him. How would you have felt in their place when Jesus not only didn't come immediately, but He delayed two extra days?

Would you have felt betrayed or as if you didn't matter to Jesus?

It is so hard to not want my way, I even tell Jesus that & He knows that, but I also tell Him I know His ways are best and beyond my understanding. I can't know the beginning & end of it all as He does

What does verse 5 say?

He loved Mary, Martha & Lazarus

Jesus' love for His three friends was as great as it had ever been, but Jesus knew what they did not. Although they didn't understand, the waiting was very important to what Jesus would ultimately do for them. What appeared to be a lack of concern was actually great love. Jesus' delay in answering laid the groundwork for an even greater miracle than healing would have been.

When Jesus finally arrived, both sisters had exactly the same response. Read John 11:21,32 (page 820).

Did you hear the hint of accusation in their statements? Their brother was dead because Jesus delayed His coming. *The knew* If He'd gotten there in time, He could have healed him.

They knew He had power to heal.
rather ironic

Have you ever blamed God for not answering your prayers the way you wanted? *Yes even when I know there is nothing lacking in Him and He is always right, I am inclined to be like Mary and feel like things are not good if it's not the way that seems so right to me*

God always has a purpose for the timing of His answer and the form of His answer. And it is always the right and best answer.

According to John 11:23-27 (page 820), what did Jesus want to make sure Mary and Martha knew? *He is Messiah, Son of God who was to come into the world from God!*

What key question did Jesus ask Martha?
Everyone who lives in me and believes in me will never ever die.
Do You Believe This Martha?

What was her answer? *"Yes Lord." "I have always believed you are the Messiah, the son of God who was to come into the world from God.*

Jesus was willing to delay His coming—even though He knew His friends would misinterpret it—because He had a far better plan that would strengthen their faith and let them know Him better.

Whatever prayer is going unanswered in your life, whatever circumstance is causing you to feel God has forgotten you, be assured that is not the truth. He has something better in store, something that will allow you to know Him more than you ever thought you could.

One day a friend entered the office of Dr. Phillips Brooks, a famous American preacher. Dr. Brooks was pacing back and forth. "What's the trouble?" the friend asked him. "The trouble?" he replied. "I'm in a hurry and God isn't. That's the trouble."

God's delays are not denials. They often teach us a greater understanding and knowledge of Him. Our trust in God is deepened, and we learn of His wisdom and patience.

We are quick to say how good God is when He answers prayer the way we ask or when something good happens to us. But is He any less good when He doesn't answer in the manner we wanted, or when He delays? Then do we say, "God is good"? And while we may not be capable of knowing what's truly best for us, God is, and He works in all our prayers and all our circumstances to bring about His good and perfect will, as we saw in chapter 4. Read Romans 8:28-29 (page 863).

⸻⸻⸻

We may not understand why God answers our prayers the way He does. But God doesn't expect us to understand, only to trust. Some day we will see the glory of God in the things we do not understand. Until then, we can trust Him, because we have learned that He is trustworthy.

Personal Reflection and Application

From this chapter,

I see... that God's ways are perfect

I believe... He loves me and His way is The right answer for me (even when I don't understand

I will... "Trust Him"

Prayer

Lord, I give my life to you. I trust in you, my God! Show me the right path; point out the road for me to follow. Lead me by your truth and teach me, for you are the God who saves me. All day long I put my hope in you (Psalm 25:1,4,5, page 424).

Thoughts, Notes, and Prayer Requests

I am so thankful that God loves me. No matter what happens I can trust Him. He will lead me by His Truth and teach me, for He is the God who saves me. All day long I put my hope in you. Please always look at me in the light of your unfailing love, for You are merciful, O LORD!

6

Alone with God

We were only a few hours into a two-and-a-half-day trip home when my widowed mother pulled her car over to the edge of the road. She turned around to where my brother, sister, and I were sitting in the backseat. "Now, kids," she said, "God has promised to supply all our needs according to His riches—and He has more riches than you can ever imagine, so we never have to worry." She took a deep breath before continuing. "I only have enough money for gas. There's no money for food or a motel, but we're not going to worry. We're going to pray." She did exactly that, right on the side of the road as cars rushed by. Then she calmly started the car up and pulled back on to the highway.

In the backseat, my siblings and I were silent as we contemplated two and a half days without food—not to mention sleeping scrunched up in the car for two nights. I shoved my hands into my pockets as I thought about what she'd just told us. To my surprise I felt a piece of paper. I pulled it out and found a ten dollar bill. We all gasped in surprise. I reached back in my pocket and found another ten dollar bill. My mom quickly pulled back off the road as I pulled out still another bill. All together I found fifty dollars in my pocket—more than enough to pay for the trip home.

I remembered my uncle hugging me goodbye that morning and

telling me not to check my pocket until we were on the road. He'd guessed my widowed mother might be short of cash. God answered my mother's prayer before she even prayed—just as He promised!

Prayer

Father, thank you for giving me rest, just as you promised. Thank you that not one word has failed of all the wonderful promises you've given me. May you be with me; may you never leave me or abandon me. May you give me the desire to do your will in everything and to obey all your commands (1 Kings 8:56-58, page 266).

Our busy lives can make it difficult to find time to pray. Full schedules crowd out our time with God. With the best of intentions, we plan to do it later in the day, but hours pass and we never get around to spending quiet time alone with God. But it's so vital to our relationship with God. In our Prayer Profile, we will look at a man whose consistent time alone with God prepared him for a terrifying circumstance.

Prayer Profile: Daniel

Background: As a youth, Daniel was taken captive by enemy soldiers and transported to their country, Babylon. In spite of his tragic circumstances, Daniel stood firm in his faith though his captors put forth intense effort to change his beliefs. God blessed Daniel, and he was eventually promoted to a position of prominence in Babylon. This made some men jealous, however, and they convinced the king to establish a decree that only allowed people to pray to the king. Whoever violated the order would be thrown into a pit of lions.

Read Daniel 6:10-14 (page 673).

What did Daniel do as soon as he learned about the law?

Went home and knelt to prayer as he always had, giving thanks

What does this passage tell you about Daniel's relationship with God?

Consistently in communication with God always thanking Him & praising Him

Read verses 15-16. What do these verses tell you about Daniel's relationship with God?

Nothing would stop him from his prayers, even the threat of death

Do your friends and co-workers know how committed you are to God?

yes & they after talk to me about concerns they have

Do you find it difficult to be open about your faith? Why?

No except when I know they are really against faith in God

Were you intrigued by the king's words to Daniel? Although King Darius does not believe in Daniel's God, he is sincerely hoping Daniel's faith is well placed. *May your God - - - rescue you*

Now read verse 17. Again, it is a case of God seemingly not answering a prayer. In spite of Daniel's faithfulness to God, in spite of his favor with the king, nothing can save him. What do you imagine Daniel's thoughts were as they pushed him inside the den and sealed a stone over the opening. Think how dark it would have been. Imagine feeling the body heat from the lions as they approached him.

What would your thoughts be?

That I'd die a horrible death but be blessed in God's presence

This is when a consistent time alone with God would be a wonderful thing to already have established. It's for precisely these kinds of storms that you need to be well fortified with God's Word prior to the storm's arrival. Daniel's intimate relationship with God would have been the only thing that could keep his sanity intact, trapped in a dark so thick you could feel it while hungry lions circle around you. But as in all the other stories we've read, God's perceived lack of response was actually a miracle in the making.

Read verses 18-23. *Darius acknowledges "God"*

Who did Daniel give the credit to?

My God sent His angels to close the lions' mouths

Don't you love the last line? *"Not a scratch!"* Why?

He was so respectful & gave all the glory to God.
Reminded the "King" I have been found innocent in God's sight and had not wronged the King

As we conclude this section, take a moment to ask God to help you trust Him more.

Time Alone with God

How do we get to know someone? By spending time with them. The more time we spend, the better we get to know them. It works the same with God. One of the ways to know Him better is through a consistent, quiet time of prayer and Bible reading.

As our Creator, God knows we're easily distracted. The more privacy we have, the less we are likely to be distracted. God wants our full attention, because He has wonderful things to share with us.

You may not have a place where you can literally close the door on all of life's distractions, but there's always a way to create a quiet place to enhance your time alone with God.

Susanna Wesley, mother of 19 children, rarely had solitude in her home. Nevertheless, she valued her time alone with God, usually spending at least an hour a day in prayer. At her appointed time she simply pulled her apron up over her head, and all her children knew not to bother their mother.

What is most likely to interfere with your daily quiet time?

I guess I have too many things to do. Also think I must answer the phone when it rings. actually I think I'm very easily distracted

What are some things you can do to resolve that issue?

I love this time w/ God so I need to pray. He'll give me wisdom and determination.

Prayer is an unlimited resource. We can bring our concerns to God whenever they arise, but it is still very important to set aside time each day to focus fully on Him.

To prepare for our prayer time, it is good to read the Bible. It tunes our hearts to God, so that we are ready to listen as He speaks to us. The listening side of our prayer time is as important as the speaking. Prayer is as essential to our relationship with God as Bible reading is.

A Bible teacher was once asked, "Which is more important, Bible reading or prayer?" He replied, "Which is more important to a bird, its right or its left wing?" They work together to keep us growing strong and balanced in Jesus.

Second Timothy 3:16-17 (page 915) lists five benefits of reading the Bible. What are they?

1. *All scripture is inspired by God and useful to: Teach us what is True.*

2. *realize what is wrong in my life*

3. *to correct when we're wrong*

4. *teach us to do what's right*

5. *Prepare & equip us to do every good work*

As you read the Bible, ask yourself questions such as

- How does this Scripture apply to my life?
- What does God want me to learn from this?

What does John 14:26 (pages 823-824) say?

I need to really rely on the Holy Spirit because He will teach me & remind me of everything God has told me in His Word!

The Holy Spirit will help you understand what you're reading. As you read the Bible, God will often prompt you to pray about things you are thankful for, sin to confess, or prayer requests to voice. One exciting way to mix Bible reading and prayer is to pray God's Word. As you read a phrase in the Bible, speak to God about it. Here is an example of how you can pray God's Word using selected phrases from Psalm 103.

> *Let all that I am praise the LORD; with my whole heart, I will praise his holy name!*
> *Let all that I am praise the LORD: may I never forget the good things he does for me.*
> *He forgives all my sins...He fills my life with good things.*

—Psalm 103:1-5 (page 460)

Example of prayer based on the Scripture:

Father, I praise you with my whole being. You are worthy of all my praise and honor. Please help me to never forget your wonderful kindness to me—all the good you do. Thank you for forgiving my sins. Thank you for the way you have provided for me.

Read the following verses and turn each into a personal prayer.

Psalm 141:3-4 (page 477)

Help me not to be negative or gossip

Psalm 150:1-2 (page 480)

I Praise God in church & in all His Wondrous mighty works & un-equaled greatness.

Philippians 4:4-7 (page 901)

Don't worry, trust Him, His peace will guard my mind & heart

1 Peter 1:3-4 (page 934)

It is often difficult to find time to be quiet and alone with God, but developing the discipline of solitude will have immeasurable impact on your life. You will be more productive and fulfilled.

Most important of all, you will become more like Jesus as you interact with people around you.

Solitude does not have to be a lengthy retreat. There can be minutes throughout our day where we can spend time alone with God. Author Donald Whitney writes,

Find ways to turn the routine into the holy, to find those "minute retreats" that can punctuate and empower even the busiest days...The busier you are, the more hectic your world, the more you need to plan daily spaces of silence and solitude. As sleep and rest are needed each day for the body, so silence and solitude are needed each day for the soul.[4]

Think about your usual schedule. When will you best be able to set aside a time of daily solitude with God?

Do whatever is necessary to develop this discipline. Do not rob yourself of what will change your life for the better!

——————— *Personal Reflection and Application* ———————

From this chapter,

I see...

I believe...

I will...

Prayer

Father, how good it is to be near you! I have made you, Sovereign Lord, my shelter, and I will tell everyone about the wonderful things you do. Teach me to wait quietly before you for my hope is in you (Psalm 73:28, page 446, and Psalm 62:5, page 440).

—— *Thoughts, Notes, and Prayer Requests* ——

Sharon - Rose-Mary
reconstruction
Lu Morse 621 - 3646

7

Praying Effectively

Gracia Burnham, who we read about earlier, reached a turning point about the tenth week of her and her husband's captivity. Angry and depressed, she wrestled with God until she realized the she "could choose to believe what God's Word says to be true whether I felt it was or not." She handed her pain and anger to the Lord. From that day on, He let her know in her spirit that He was still faithful.

Throughout her horrible ordeal of fear, illness, and near-starvation, Gracia fought discouragement with prayer. She was frustrated with praying for release, so she said to her husband, Martin, "Okay, I'm going to pray for something else: a hamburger! The only way for us to get a hamburger is to get out of her, right?"

In a very unusual way, God got them out of the jungle for a short period of time and even provided hamburgers. They knew God had the power to do anything. He could release them at any time. They realized that He wanted them there for a reason.

After over a year in captivity, rescuers reached the Burnhams. Gracia was shot in the leg, but she survived. Martin was killed during the rescue. God heard the Burnhams' prayers and those of many who faithfully prayed for them, and He answered those prayers. The answer was not always what they expected or even wanted, but they trusted Him.[5]

How do you respond when God's answer to prayer is a difficult one?

Prayer

Lord, let me live in a way that will honor and please you, so that my life will produce every kind of good fruit. Let me grow as I learn to know you better and better (Colossians 1:10, page 902).

In our last chapter we discussed the importance of daily solitude. It's during those times that we come to know God more intimately and learn to recognize His voice giving us direction for our lives. In our Prayer Profile this week we will read about a man who learned to listen to God and as a result, the direction of his life changed forever.

Prayer Profile: Samuel

Background: Hannah, Samuel's mother, dedicated her son to God's service at his birth. He was raised in the temple by Eli the priest.

Read 1 Samuel 3:1-10 (page 213).

How many times did God call Samuel? *4 times*

Samuel wasn't used to hearing God's voice, so it took a while for him to realize it was God. It even took a while for his spiritual mentor, Eli, to realize it was God.

God speaks today in many ways. As we are attuned to Him and are spending time with Him, we hear Him speak through His Word, prayer, the Holy Spirit, and the people around us. Have you ever felt like God was clearly impressing something on you?

yes

How did you respond? *do it now*

How did Samuel finally respond? *here I am*

Read verses 11-18.

Samuel's first assignment from God was an extremely difficult one, wasn't it? Imagine being a boy and delivering such a devastating message to your spiritual mentor. However, if you read the chapters prior to this one, you'll see that Eli had been lax in both his spiritual leadership of the people and in parenting his sons. God had warned him about it, but Eli didn't listen. Do you think Eli might have suspected what Samuel was going to say? Do you think that could be why he spoke so harshly to Samuel—to give him courage to speak truthfully what God had told him? *yes*

Have you ever struggled with something God has asked you to
do or say?

How did Eli respond to Samuel's message? *Gracefully*

It's very sad, isn't it? There is no anger or outrage in his response,
because he knew he was guilty of ignoring God's loving guidance,
and now he would face the consequences he'd brought on himself
and his sons.

Read verses 19-21.

Did Samuel follow in Eli's footsteps? *Not the disobedient part*

Eli helped Samuel learn to discern God's voice. He helped him
learn to speak God's word to the Israelites with courage. Verse 20
is significant. What does it say?

Everyone knew Samuel was God's prophet. People recognize when someone is a faithful follower of God. There is a difference about them that people respond to and respect. We can have no higher personal goal than to live in a way so that everyone—Christian or not—respects our faithful walk with God.

Eight Principles of Effective Prayer

Principle #1: Walking in God's Will

Prayer should never be seen as a means of getting God to do our will, but instead aligning our will with His. Read 1 John 5:13-15 (pages 943-944).

What gives us the confidence to know God will answer our prayers? *If we ask according to His will*

How does Romans 12:2 (page 866) describe the will of God? *Let God transform me into a new person by changing the way we think. Then you will learn to know God's will for you, which is good, pleasing & perfect*

There is nothing to fear about God's will, because it is good and pleasing and perfect. Knowing this, why would we want to be anywhere but in the center of God's will? That's where our prayers are answered. That's where we access the power of God that changes lives around us.

2 jars ① good things ② God can, you can't

But how do we walk in God's will? What did the first part of this verse say? *Don't copy the behaviour customs of the world*

As we read and meditate on Scripture, and as we pray and remain yielded to God, He transforms our lives. He changes the way we think! As our thought process changes, so will our behavior. We will become a more and more accurate reflection of Jesus. David put it this way in Psalm 51:10 (page 436), *"Create in me a clean heart, O God. Renew a loyal spirit within me."* I'm so thankful we can call on God to shape and reshape our lives through the power of His Word.

Read Colossians 1:9 (page 902).

How might you pray for someone desiring to be in God's will?

Keep praying

God's will is not a secret! He wants us to understand it. If we read the Bible and ask God to give us knowledge of His will, He will answer.

What does Colossians 1:10 (page 902) say will be the result of understanding God's will?

will honor & please God

Doesn't that sound wonderful—to learn to live in a way that always honors and pleases God? Don't you want to learn to know God better and better? It's not always easy. But there is purpose and meaning in living in God's will.

Jesus set an example for us of being willing to do God's will. Read Luke 22:42 (page 805).

What did Jesus pray? *not my will but yours*

His submission to God's will was without reservation, wasn't it? Regardless of the cost, He wanted to be in God's will. But think of this. Every person who has ever lived can be a beneficiary of Jesus' submission to God's will. And when we submit to God's will, other people will benefit!

Even though we know God's will is the best possible way to live, we still often try to convince God to do things our way, don't we? God understands our self-centered inclination and will help us.

What does it say in Philippians 2:13 (page 900)? *God is working in you/me giving me the desire & the power to do whats pleasing to Him*

Principle #2: Walking in Faith

What do the following verses say about prayer?

Matthew 21:22 (page 752)

Mark 11:22-24 (page 772) *you can pray for huge, unimmaginable miracles & don't doubt*

What do these verses say to you?

We can see the vital part faith plays in our prayers. Our faith accesses God's power.

What is the first thing James 1:6-8 (page 930) says about faith?

We can very easily get faith in ourselves mixed up with faith in God. Ego is a subtle and insidious enemy to our faith in God. We need to continually acknowledge our complete dependency on God.

It is not great faith that God requires, but faith in a great God.

What is the next thing it says?

Dont waver

When we mix an attitude of self-sufficiency in with our faith in God, we become ineffective. And the result is awful. What do verses 7 and 8 say?

Do you ever feel unstable or unsettled? After reading these verses, what do you think might be at the root of such feelings?

What can you do to change this?

When we incorporate faith into our prayers, we trust God to do what He has promised. Doubting God's promise erodes our ability to believe.

Principle #3: Walking in Obedience

> What are some principles for effective prayer found in 1 John 3:22 (pages 942-943) and Micah 6:8 (page 706)?

An example of applying these principles is found in the following story:

> Tim was 15 years old, and all his friends were going to spend the day at a nearby beach. He asked his father for permission to go. His father told Tim he didn't want him to go, because of a special family dinner planned that day. However, he told Tim he could make up his own mind about what to do.
>
> Tim understood the importance of the family dinner, but he really wanted to go to the beach more and that was the decision he made. The family was just sitting down for dinner when, to his father's delight, in walked Tim.
>
> "I thought you decided to go to the beach," his father exclaimed.
>
> "I did," Tim replied, "but then I realized how important this was to you, so I came back."

In the end, Tim chose to do what was right by putting his father's desire above his own. In doing so, he aligned himself fully with his father's will, and therefore his father's blessing.

Principle #4: Remaining in God

Read John 15:7 (page 824) and note what it says.

when you remain in me & my words

To remain in God is to live in uninterrupted fellowship with God and in complete dependence on Him. How do you think we can do this?

By praying to Him for His will will be done in me

What is the second condition in this verse?

my words remain in you → you can ask for anything you want & it will be granted

How can God's Word remain in you?

be faithful to read, meditate & try to follow His Word

"Prayer is powerful. We rest on the relationship and faith that is built when we live our lives as people of prayer. Still, prayer without obedience is incomplete. As we are brought into places of prayer, places of entrusting our lives and circumstances to God— yes, in this dialogue of the deepest communion— He speaks. He asks us to respond to His leading. As followers of Jesus Christ, we dutifully and delightfully obey, knowing that His greater aim is for our good."

—*Cheryl Lee Davis*

This involves more than just reading the Bible. It means meditating on it, applying it to your life, and allowing it to regulate and control your behavior.

When we remain in God and His Word, our requests will be in harmony with His will. That's when we can have complete confidence that He will answer our prayers.

Principle #5: Keeping a Pure Heart

> Read Psalm 66:18 (page 442).
>
> What effect does sin have on our prayer? *Closes the contact w/ God*

Now read Proverbs 28:13 (page 501) to see how we can restore our communication with God.

> What are the two things we need to do?
>
> 1. *Confess sin*
>
> 2. *Stop sin, turn away from sin*

Confession alone isn't enough. You have to turn away from the behavior or attitude that is sinful.

Principle #6: Have a Sincere Motive

When we pray, our motives are to be sincere. This is the next principle of effective prayer. Read James 4:3 (page 932).

Motives

That last phrase says it all, doesn't it? What is at the root of all wrong motives? *God based or me based*

We have to constantly guard against our selfishness. It will always be creeping in to crowd God out. Why are you praying for something? What is your hoped-for result? Is it self-based or pleasing God-based? Be constantly on guard to keep your heart and motive pure.

Principle #7: Have a Forgiving Heart

Read Colossians 3:12-13 (pages 903-904).

Why are we supposed to forgive?

God commands we forgive — also He forgave us when we didn't deserve

This is a difficult principle for some to accept—especially if you've been grievously wronged by someone. But the truth is, if your heart is filled with bitterness or resentment, there is limited room for God's action. God is rich in mercy, and because His love is so great, you can let go of what you are harboring against someone.

There is a parable in Matthew 18:21-35 (page 749) that paints a vivid picture of how abhorrent our unforgiveness is to God. Note the main points.

continue to forgive, again & again. God has forgiven us so much how can we withhold grace & forgiveness. God will punish me if I refuse to forgive others from my heart

If you are struggling to forgive someone, stop and look at the injustice Jesus endured. No one suffered more than He did. He understands exactly how hard it is for you to let go of your feelings of betrayal; but if you ask, He will help you. The freedom you experience will far outweigh the sometimes difficult experience of letting go.

Principle #8: Be Concerned for Others

Read Luke 10:25-37 (page 792) and Philippians 2:4 (page 900). Walking in harmony with God will always have an outward focus. He wants us to be responsive to the needs of people around us. What are some ways you *take an interest* in the people around you?

> *Luke*
> *Inherit eternal life*
> *Love God w/ all heart & neighbor as self.*
> *Neighbor — The one who shows mercy*
> *when sees the need*
>
> *Phil. Don't only look out for own interests.*
>
> *Take an interest in others too:*
> *Those who need a friend — be caring*
> *those " " food & shelter — be generous —*
> *those who are sick visit & keep in touch.*
> *Notice those who are sad & down or mistreated.*
> *Be a friend, care, help*

Become familiar with the eight principles of effective prayer that we've discussed. Perhaps you can focus on a different one each week until it is incorporated into your life.

In John 14:13 (page 823), Jesus says, *"You can ask for anything in my name, and I will do it, so that the Son can bring glory to the Father."* The reason we pray is so that God will be glorified. The way we pray and the way He answers all bring Him glory.

———— *Personal Reflection and Application* ————

From this chapter,

I see... how I need to pray for the people I encounter in Jesus' name to bring glory to God.

I believe... God Will answer and bring Glory to the Father

I will... endeavor to my heart and hands even more than I have

∾

✗ *Prayer*

Father, help me to let go of all bitterness, rage, anger, harsh words, and slander, as well as all types of evil behavior. Instead, help me to be kind to everyone around me, tenderhearted, forgiving them, just as you, through Christ, have forgiven me (Ephesians 4:31-32, page 897). See yellow tag

———— *Thoughts, Notes, and Prayer Requests* ————

Father I Thank you so much for working in my heart on these issues over the years & even this past year. Please help me be ever more aware of what you want/require from me. Father please keep me from all bitterness, rage, anger, harshwords and slander as well as all types of evil behavior. Instead help me be kind, tenderhearted, forgiving just as you through Christ has forgiven me

8

A Pattern for Prayer

Rosalind and Jonathan Goforth were missionaries in China. Because of a dangerous uprising in the country, they were ordered to return home immediately. They escaped with their lives, but lost all of their possessions. As they waited in Shanghai for the ship home, Rosalind tried to replace their lost clothing. Alone in a strange city and knowing no one, she wondered how she would ever be able to make enough clothing for their children to wear on the long trip.

She knelt, asking God to send someone to help her. While still on her knees, she heard a knock at the door. Opening it, she found two women who were complete strangers. They'd seen the Goforths' name on a list of refugees and felt moved by God to offer their assistance. The three women worked together and sewed enough clothes for the children to last the trip.

After her new friends were gone, Rosalind discovered that she'd neglected to make anything for the baby. Once again she knelt and asked for God's help. They got on the ship for home, but while they were docked in Japan a package was brought to their stateroom marked with her name. Someone had thrown it on the deck. Rosalind opened the package to find a supply of baby clothes that exactly fit her baby. With the package was a letter from a missionary in Japan who had lost her child. God had directed her to give these clothes to Rosalind.

There are no impossible situations for God. He delights in answering our prayers!

Prayer

Father, I pray that I will be strengthened with all your glorious power, so I will have all the endurance and patience I need. May I be filled with joy, always thanking you, my Father. Thank you for enabling me to share in the inheritance that belongs to your people, who live in the light (Colossians 1:11-12, page 902).

Prayer Profile: Jesus

Background: Jesus is living out His final days on earth. He knows the horror He'll soon be enduring, but His concern is not for Himself—it is for His beloved disciples He will be leaving behind. For several years now, Jesus has worked closely with them, teaching them to live in the power of God and equipping them to teach others. Now the time for teaching has ended, and He is praying for them.

Read John 17:1-26 (pages 825-826). For a more complete background, you could first read John 13–16 (pages 822-825).

Who is the focus of His prayer in John 17:1-5 (page 825)?

God the Father

Who is the focus of His prayer in John 17:6-19 (page 825)?

Those God the Father had given Jesus) Followers) Disciples) and those in the future

Who is the focus of His prayer in John 17:20-26 (pages 825-826)?

Me > Us > all who will ever believe

Does it amaze you to realize that, at such a time as this, Jesus prayed for *you*! You were on His mind, just as His disciples were—because He loved you. The prayer He prayed is so very personal. What is He asking God for in verse 21?

Unity among those who are His, believers > Christians

Do you realize the implication of His prayer? Jesus and God are one Being. There is no division between them. *Jesus wants that same closeness for us*, and because His blood takes away our sin, it is possible. What does this mean to you?

In God we can really love eachother and have "one mind in Christ" The love & unity only He can give us

What does Jesus pray in verse 23?

Our perfect unity will show the world He is in His followers (Us/me) He wants the world to know Him through our unity

Imagine the depths of love that Christ has for us! He wants God to love us with the same intensity that God loves Jesus! Incredible!

What is Jesus praying for in verse 24? *That we will be in heaven with Him See The Glory of God.*

Jesus actually prayed for you and me! He wants everyone to spend eternity with Him.

Read John 17 each day this week. You'll be amazed at the different ways God speaks to you each day. When a verse is particularly meaningful, copy it onto a notecard and memorize it.

Teach Us to Pray

Have you ever wondered why, if Jesus is God, He had to pray? It's not that He *had* to pray, but that He *wanted* to pray, *needed* to pray— to stay closely connected to His Father. And every part of His life on earth was an example for us. While on earth He lived in dependence upon God as an example to us. He made prayer a priority as an example to us.

One day His disciples asked Jesus to teach them to pray. The pattern He gave them is commonly known as "The Lord's Prayer," and it is actually a great model prayer for disciples (Christ-followers).

Read it in Matthew 6:9-13 (page 737), and then we'll look at it phrase by phrase.

"Our Father in heaven." The Jews rarely called God by the name Father before Jesus came. In this prayer, Jesus calls God "Father." And He tells us to pray the same way. God wants us to speak to Him in a personal way—as a child to his or her father.

Jesus also reminds us that our Father is in heaven. He is exalted high above the earth and is supreme, holy, and almighty! He is to be respected and revered. As we learn who God is, our trust in Him develops and our dependence upon Him deepens.

Pg 737, Matt 6:9b

"May your name be kept holy." What do you think is the purpose of the second phrase of verse nine?

Also my part in keeping Gods name Holy, exalted, respected, supreme, almighty, revered!

It is important to never forget God's holiness. In this pattern, Jesus taught us to acknowledge God's holiness when we pray. Imagine if we wrote, *"May your name be kept holy"* over every plan we made, over our daily schedule, and over every activity and choice of entertainment.

How different would your choices and decisions be if your measuring stick was to keep God's name holy?

Hungering and thursting for His righteousness and always living by His Word & Praying > Constant contact

One way to honor God is through our prayers. Write a prayer below that honors God's holy name. If you're not sure how to do it, here is an example:

> Father, I honor your holy name.
> May your name be revered and worshiped.
> May your name be honored in my life—
> my thoughts, my words, my attitudes, and all that I do.
> May I praise your name forever and ever.

Keep my thoughts pure

Father I praise & honor your holy name may all who love you bring honor to you. I thank and praise you that you give us your faith, to know and believe that in you is life. You are so wonderful beyond my understanding, you knew me and made me in my mother. You also knew she would tell me about you! Please help me honor you & her by passing on the good news of faith and the life only you can give those who love you. I love you, may my life, thoughts, attitudes and all I do bring praise & honor to your name.

"May your Kingdom come soon." With this statement Jesus references God's Kingdom.

Read Luke 17:20-21 (pages 799-800), and note where the Kingdom of God is. *It is not by visable signs. The Kingdom of God is already among you. Kingdom of God within*

What does Colossians 1:11-14 (page 902) say about God's Kingdom? *He will strengthen me w/ his glorious power so I will have the endurance & patience I need. "May you be filled w/ joy always thanking the Father that He has rescued us from the kingdom of darkness & put us into the Kingdom of of his dear Son, who purchased our freedom & forgave our sins.*

A kingdom indicates a king on the throne. When we surrender to Jesus, He becomes King of our lives. We allow Him to be on the throne of our hearts and in charge of our lives.

Jesus spoke of the Kingdom as being in the present, as well as the future. In Revelation 11:15 (page 955) it says, *"The world has now become the Kingdom of our Lord and of his Christ, and he will reign forever and ever."*

"May your will be done on earth as it is in heaven." When we seek God's purpose in our prayers, our hearts are aligned with His will. Then we begin to see God at work in our lives. Again, Jesus set the example for us of staying aligned with His Father's will.

What does John 5:30 (page 813) say? *We can do nothing on our own. We judge as God tells us, so our judgement is just because we carry out the will of God the father not my own will.*

Read Hebrews 13:20-21 (page 929). What does verse 21 tell us?

may God equip you with all you need for doing His will. May He produce in you thru the power of Jesus Christ, every good thing that is pleasing to Him

God equips us to do His will! He doesn't expect us to do it on our own. Isn't that incredible? And how does it say we will be able to do what pleases Him?

By His Power we can do every good thing that pleases Him. It's the only way we can do it.

In no way are we ever on our own in our efforts to honor God. God makes every possible provision for us to be obedient in our faith walk. Does that fill you with overwhelming gratitude? Write your thoughts below.

I am so thankful that I am His child and He will give me power to live & do what He desires

Have you noticed that so far there have been no personal pronouns in Jesus' example of prayer? He makes God the focus, not the person praying. It is not about what we want, but rather about God's perfect plan and His ultimate desires. The first half of the prayer is designed to focus only on God and align our will with His. But even as He moves into personal prayer requests, He never prays just for Himself, He always includes others.

"Give us today the food we need." Every area of our life is important to God. Our physical, mental, and spiritual well-being are all important to Him. Sometimes we are so concerned with our material needs

that we overlook His willingness to provide for our emotional and spiritual needs. We can depend on God to provide all of them for us. There is no limit to His resources. God is the source of every blessing.

Read Matthew 6:25-32 (pages 737-738).

According to this passage, what do we have to worry about?

Nothing: Our heavenly Father already knows our needs

Concern?

God has promised to take care of us, but sometimes we don't give Him the opportunity. Instead we spend the bulk of our time and money taking care of ourselves, instead of focusing on God and others. He wants us to depend on Him each day to provide for our needs.

Read Philippians 4:19 (page 901).

What do you think the word "all" includes? *All > everything*
Lest I forget - - -
Everything I need including emotional, spiritual, physical, financial, attitude, whatever

That says it all. There is no need God will not supply when we take them to Him in prayer. David put it this way in Psalm 37:25 (page 430):

Once I was young, and now I am old. Yet I have never seen the godly abandoned or their children begging for bread.

And James reminds us that God is the giver of every good and perfect gift. He supplies our needs and He gives good gifts to His children (James 1:17, page 930).

Every good and perfect thing! Whatever God supplies for us will be right.

"And forgive us our sins, as we have forgiven those who sin against us."
We've already addressed the importance of forgiveness, and Jesus again stressed its importance in His example of how we are to pray.

But remember this. When you find it difficult to forgive, God has promised to give you whatever you need. If you need the strength to forgive someone, ask God for it. He will not fail you!

"And don't let us yield to temptation, but rescue us from the evil one."
God doesn't tempt us, but He allows temptations and trials, because they are part of our learning process. He allows us to be put into situations where our faith is tested and strengthened. However, even in this we are not expected to handle it alone.

Read 1 Corinthians 10:13 (page 876), and note what it says.

The temptations in my life are not unique and God is faithful to make me strong and not allow the temptation to overpower me. He will show me a way out so I can go on

What four points does it make about the temptations we face?

1. *Same as others face*

2. *God is faithful*

3. *He will not allow the temptation to be more than you can stand.*

4. *When you are tempted, he will show you a way out so that you can endure.*

Don't you love the second point—that God is faithful? Really, that's all we need to know, isn't it? He is faithful and He will help us make the right decision.

There is another verse that helps us when facing temptation. Read 2 Timothy 1:7 (page 914). Because Jesus lives in us, we have His power flowing through us. There's no need to be afraid, because His self-control is at work in us! *God has not given us a Spirit of fear*

Have you ever felt God giving you the strength to do something you felt you couldn't do otherwise? What was the outcome?

I was able to do it though it wasn't easy it led to pleasure and satisfaction in my life and I knew it was pleasing to God.

choir / Di

|||||||||||||||||||||||

So here we are at the end of our study on prayer. What part of the study has had the strongest impact on your life?

Constant reminder to stay in God's Word and in touch with Him in prayer

I hope you will never take for granted the wonderful privilege we have to connect with God through prayer. I hope you will never lose the sense of wonder that in one of Jesus' last prayers He prayed on earth, He prayed for you. Be confident in the truth that God desires to remain connected with you in prayer (John 15:3-5, page 824).

Remain in Me & I will remain in you

For our conclusion, let's look up one final verse. Read Revelation 5:13 (page 952). What does it say will happen one day?

Every Creature will Praise Him

Imagine that day when every living creature and person will all pray the very same prayer: *"Blessing and honor and glory and power belong to the one sitting on the throne and to the Lamb forever and ever."* What an incredible experience that will be!

— *Personal Reflection and Application* —

From this chapter,

I see... God's complete love for us and the complete provision to live this life for Him/His way, that He gives —

I believe... I can live a loving, caring, forgiving life putting others before myself if I let his word and Spirit dwell in me *richly!*

I will... dedicate my time and energy toward this goal so that I might bless others and perhaps guide others to believe Him and receive Him & the forgiveness only He can give

Prayer

Father, I will exalt you, my God and King, and praise your name forever and ever. I will praise you every day; yes, I will praise you forever. Great are you Lord! You are most worthy of praise! No one can measure your greatness...I will meditate on your majestic, glorious splendor and your wonderful miracles. Your awe-inspiring deeds will be on my tongue; I will proclaim your greatness. I will share the story of your wonderful goodness; I will sing with joy about your righteousness (Psalm 145:1-7, page 478).

Thoughts, Notes, and Prayer Requests

Thank you Lord

Jena
707-367-5945

Journal Pages

Prayer

Worship, Praise, and Giving Thanks to God

> *Worship the LORD in all his holy splendor.*
> *Let all the earth tremble before him.*
>
> —Psalm 96:9 (page 458)

> *Give thanks to the LORD and proclaim his greatness.*
> *Let the whole world know what he has done.*
> *Sing to him; yes, sing his praises.*
> *Tell everyone about his wonderful deeds.*
> *Exult in his holy name;*
> *rejoice, you who worship the LORD.*
>
> —Psalm 105:1-3 (page 461)

_____

_____

_____

_____

_____

Confession

Have mercy on me, O God, because of your unfailing love.
Because of your great compassion, blot out the stain of my sins. Wash me
clean from my guilt. Purify me from my sin…
Create in me a clean heart, O God.
Renew a loyal spirit within me.

—Psalm 51:1-2,10 (page 436)

_____

_____

_____

_____

_____

_____

_____

_____

_____

_____

_____

_____

_____

_____

_____

_____

_____

Asking and Intercession

Pray in the Spirit at all times and on every occasion.
Stay alert and be persistent in your prayers for
all believers everywhere.

—Ephesians 6:18 (page 898)

_____

_____

_____

_____

_____

_____

_____

_____

_____

_____

_____

_____

_____

_____

_____

_____

_____

_____

_____

_____

_____

_____

_____

Know God

It does not matter what has happened in your past. No matter what you've done, no matter how you've lived your life,

God is personally interested in you right now.
He cares about you.

God understands your frustration, your loneliness, your heart-aches. He wants each of us to come to Him, to know Him personally.

God is so <u>rich in mercy</u>, and he <u>loved us so</u> much,
that even though we were dead because of our sins,
he gave us life when he raised Christ from the dead.
(It is only by God's grace that you have been saved!)
—Ephesians 2:4-5 (page 895)

God loves you.

He created you in His image. His desire is to be in relationship with you. He wants you to belong to Him.

Sadly, our sin gets in the way. It separates us from God, and without Him we are dead in our spirits. There is nothing we can do to close that gap. There is nothing we can do to give ourselves life. No matter how well we may behave.

But God loves us so much that He made a way to eliminate that gap and give us new life, His kind of life—to restore the relationship. His love for us is so great, so tremendous, that He sent Jesus Christ, His only Son, to earth to live, and then die—filling the gap and taking the punishment we deserve for refusing God's ways.

God made Christ, who never sinned, to be the offering for our sin, so that we could be made right with God through Christ.

—*2 Corinthians 5:21 (page 884)*

Jesus Christ, God's Son, not only died to pay the penalty for your sin, but He conquered death when He rose from the grave. He is ready to share His life with you.

Christ reconciles us to God. Jesus is alive today. He will give you a new beginning and a newly created life when you surrender control of your life to Him.

Anyone who belongs to Christ has become a new person. The old life is gone; a new life has begun!

—*2 Corinthians 5:17 (page 884)*

How do you begin this new life? You need to realize

…the necessity of repenting from sin and turning to God, and of having faith in our Lord Jesus.

—*Acts 20:21 (page 849)*

Agree with God about your sins and believe that Jesus came to save you, that He is your Savior and Lord. Ask Him to lead your life.

God loved the world so much that he gave his one and only Son,
so that everyone who believes in him will not perish but have
eternal life. God sent his Son into the world not to judge the
world, but to save the world through him.

—*John 3:16-17 (page 811)*

Pray something like this:

*Jesus, I do believe you are the Son of God and that you died on
the cross to pay the penalty for my sin. I agree with you about
my sin and I want to live a life that pleases you. Enter my life as
my Savior and Lord.*

I want to follow you and make you the leader of my life.

*Thank you for your gift of eternal life and for the Holy Spirit,
who has now come to live in me. I ask this in your name. Amen.*

God puts His Spirit inside you, who enables you to live a life pleasing to Him. He gives you new life that will never die, that will last forever—eternally.

When you surrender your life to Jesus Christ, you are making the most important decision of your life. Stonecroft would like to offer you a free download of *A New Beginning*, a short Bible study that will help you as you begin your new life in Christ. Go to **stonecroft.org/newbeginning.**

If you'd like to talk with someone right now about this prayer, call **1.888.NEED.HIM.**

Who Is Stonecroft?
Connecting women with God, each other, and their communities.

Every day Stonecroft communicates the Gospel in meaningful ways. Whether through a speaker sharing her transformational story, or side by side in a ministry service project, the Gospel of Jesus Christ goes forward. In one-on-one conversations with a long-term friend, and through well-developed online and print resources, the Gospel of Jesus Christ goes forward.

For nearly 75 years, we've been introducing women to Jesus Christ and training them to share His Good News with others.

Stonecroft understands and appreciates the influence of one woman's life. When you reach her, you touch everyone she knows—her family, friends, neighbors, and co-workers. The real Truth of the Gospel brings real redemption into real lives.

Our life-changing, faith-building community resources include:

- *Stonecroft Bible and Book Studies*—both topical and traditional chapter-by-chapter studies. Stonecroft studies are designed for those in small groups—those who know Christ and those who do not yet know Him—to simply yet profoundly discover God's Word together.

- *Outreach Events and Service Activities*—set the stage for women to be encouraged and equipped to hear and share the Gospel with their communities. Whether in a large venue, workshop, or small group setting, women are prepared to serve their communities with the love of Christ.

- *Small Group Studies for Christians*—these studies engage believers in God's heart for those who do not know Him. Our most recent, the Aware Series, includes *Aware, Belong,* and *Call.*

- *Stonecroft Life Publications*—clearly explain the Gospel through stories of people whose lives have been transformed by Jesus Christ.

- *Stonecroft Prayer*—foundational for everything we do, prayer groups, materials, and training set the focus on our reliance on God for all ministry and to share the Gospel.

- *Stonecroft's Website*—stonecroft.org—offering fresh content daily to equip and encourage you.

Dedicated and enthusiastic Stonecroft staff serve you via Divisional Field Directors stationed across the United States, and a Home Office team overseeing the leadership of tens of thousands of dedicated volunteers worldwide.

Visit **stonecroft.org** to learn more about these and other outstanding Stonecroft resources, groups, and events.

Contact us via **connections@stonecroft.org** or **800.525.8627.**

STONECROFT
stonecroft.org

Books for Further Study

|||||||||||||||||||||||||||||

Briscoe, Jill. *Prayer That Works*. Carol Stream, IL: Tyndale House Publishers, 2000.

Burnham, Gracia. *In the Presence of My Enemies*. Carol Stream, IL: Tyndale House Publishers, 2003.

Jeremiah, David. *Prayer, the Great Adventure*. Sisters, OR: Multnomah Publishers, 1997.

Dean, Jennifer Kennedy. *Heart's Cry: Principles of Prayer*. Birmingham, AL: New Hope Publishers, 2007.

Glaspey, Terry. *25 Keys to Life-Changing Prayer*. Eugene, OR: Harvest House Publishers, 2010.

Lucado, Max. *Experiencing the Heart of Jesus*. Nashville, TN: Thomas Nelson Publishers, 2003.

MacArthur, John. *Lord, Teach Me to Pray*. Nashville, TN: J. Countryman, 2003.

Murray, Andrew. *With Christ in the School of Prayer*. City unavailable: Trinity Press, 2012.

Whitney, Donald S. *Spiritual Disciplines for the Christian Life*. Colorado Springs, CO: NavPress, 1991.

Yancey, Philip. *Prayer: Does It Make Any Difference?* Grand Rapids, MI: Zondervan, 2006.

Stonecroft Resources

||||||||||||||||||||||||||||||

Stonecroft Bible Studies make the Word of God accessible to everyone. These studies allow small groups to discover the adventure of a personal relationship with God and introduce others to God's unlimited love, grace, forgiveness, and power. To learn more, visit stonecroft.org/biblestudies.

Who Is Jesus? (6 chapters)
He was a rebel against the status quo. The religious community viewed Him as a threat. The helpless and outcast considered Him a friend. Explore the life and teachings of Jesus—this rebel with a cause who challenges us today to a life of radical faith.

What Is God Like? (6 chapters)
What is God like? Is He just a higher power? Has He created us and left us on our own? Where is He when things don't make sense? Discover what the Bible tells us about God and how we can know Him in a life-transforming way.

Who Is the Holy Spirit? (6 chapters)
Are you living up to the full life that God wants for you? Learn about the Holy Spirit, our Helper and power source for everyday living, who works in perfect harmony with God the Father and Jesus the Son.

Connecting with God (8 chapters)
Prayer is our heart-to-heart communication with our heavenly Father. This study examines the purpose, power, and elements of prayer, sharing biblical principles for effective prayer.

Today I Pray

When we bow before God on behalf of someone who doesn't yet know of His saving work, of His great love in sending His Son, Jesus, of His mercy and goodness, we enter into a work that has eternal impact. Stonecroft designed *Today I Pray* as a 30-day intercessory prayer commitment that you may use to focus your prayers on behalf of a specific person, or to pray for many—because your prayers are powerful and important!

Prayer Worth Repeating (15 devotions)

There is no place where your prayers to the one and only God cannot penetrate, no circumstance prayers cannot impact. As the mother of adult children, your greatest influence into their lives is through prayer. *Prayer Worth Repeating* is a devotional prayer guide designed to focus your prayers and encourage you to trust God more deeply as He works in the lives of your adult children.

Pray & Play Devotional (12 devotions)

It's playgroup with a purpose! Plus Mom tips. For details on starting a Pray & Play group, visit **stonecroft.org/prayandplay or call 800.525.8627.**

Prayer Journal

A practical resource to strengthen your prayer life, this booklet includes an introductory section about the importance of prayer, the basic elements of prayer and a clear Gospel presentation, as well as 40 pages of journaling your prayer requests and God's answers.

Ready to Pray

Gail shares how to develop and build a powerful prayer life and live out your personal testimony of a life transformed by the power of prayer and a heart of worship.

The Call of the Sandpiper

Meryl leads you on a journey with God through these 52 inspiring devotionals. During your quiet times with Jesus, He will prepare you for the week ahead and bring you closer to Him, your loving Savior. Meryl will inspire you to step off the beach and into God's potential for you!

Prayer—Talking with God

This booklet provides insight and biblical principles to help you establish a stronger, more effective prayer life.

Aware (5 lessons)

Making Jesus known every day starts when we are *Aware* of those around us. This dynamic Stonecroft Small Group Bible Study about "Always Watching and Responding with Encouragement" equips and engages people in the initial steps to the joys of evangelism.

Belong (6 lessons)

For many in today's culture, the desire to belong is often part of their journey to believe. *Belong* explores how we can follow in Jesus' footsteps—and walk with others on their journey to belong.

Call (7 lessons)

Every day we meet people without Christ. That is God's intention. He wants His people to initiate and build friendships. He wants us together. *Call* helps us take a closer look at how God makes Himself known through our relationships with those around us.

Discover together God's clear calling for you and those near to you.

Order these and other Stonecroft Resources at our online store at **stonecroft.org/store.**

If you have been encouraged and brought closer to God by this study, please consider giving a gift to Stonecroft so that others can experience life change as well. You can find information about giving online at **stonecroft.org.** (Click on the "Donate" tab.)

If you'd like to give via telephone, please contact us at **800.525.8627.** Or you can mail your gift to

Stonecroft
PO Box 9609
Kansas City, MO 64134-0609

STONECROFT

PO Box 9609, Kansas City, MO 64134-0609
Telephone: 816.763.7800 | 800.525.8627 | Fax: 816.765.2522
E-mail: connections@stonecroft.org | stonecroft.org

Abundant Life Bible
New Living Translation
Holy Bible

*Experience the presence of God
in everyday life*

Stonecroft is pleased to partner with
Tyndale to offer the New Living
Translation Holy Bible as the
companion for our newly released
Stonecroft Bible Studies.

The New Living Translation translators set out to render the message of the original
Scripture language texts into clear, contemporary English. In this *translation*, scholars kept
the concerns of both formal-equivalence and dynamic-equivalence in mind. Their
goal was a Bible that is faithful to the ancient texts and eminently readable.
The result is a translation that is both accurate and powerful.

TRUTH MADE CLEAR

Features of the Abundant Life Bible

- Features are easy-to-use and written
  for people who don't yet know Jesus
  Christ personally.

- Unequaled clarity and accuracy

- Dictionary included

- Concordance included

- Old Testament included

- Introductory notes on important abundant life
  topics such as:
  - Gospel presentation   Practical guidance
  - Joy   Life's tough issues
  - Peace   Prayer

- Insights from a relationship with Jesus Christ.

- Ideal Scripture text for those not familiar with
  the Bible!

Notes

1. This amazing answer to prayer was experienced by Stonecroft staffer Jeff Zogg.

2. Adapted from *Living Church, Bible Expositor and Illuminator* quote, as found at www.moreillustrations.com/illustrations/prayer%2014.html.

3. Gracia Burnham, *In the Presence of My Enemies* (Carol Stream, IL: Tyndale House Publishers, 2003), pages 233, 238.

4. Donald S. Whitney, *Spiritual Disciplines for the Christian Life* (Colorado Springs, CO: NavPress, 1991), pages 195, 199.

5. Burnham, pages 142-143, 238, 242, 262-263, 301-302.

6. Rosalind Goforth, *How I Know God Answers Prayer* (Glen Marais, South Africa: CruGuru, 2008), page 35